Finding Advice
from the Internet
for the Older
Generation

Other Books of Interest

*****

Finding Advice from the Internet for the Older Generation

Jim Gatenby

BERNARD BABANI (publishing) LTD
The Grampians
Shepherds Bush Rd
London W6 7NF
England

www.babanibooks.com

Please Note

Although every care has been taken with the production of this book to ensure that any projects, designs, modifications and/or programs, etc., contained herewith, operate in a correct and safe manner and also that any components specified are normally available in Great Britain, the Publishers and Author do not accept responsibility in any way for the failure (including fault in design) of any project, design, modification or program to work correctly or to cause damage to any equipment that it may be connected to or used in conjunction with, or in respect of any other damage or injury that may be so caused, nor do the Publishers accept responsibility in any way for the failure to obtain specified components.

Notice is also given that if equipment that is still under warranty is modified in any way or used or connected with home-built equipment then that warranty may be void.

First Published - April 2005

British Library Cataloguing in Publication Data:

A catalogue record for this book is available from the British Library

ISBN 0 85934 607 2

Cover Design by Gregor Arthur

Printed and bound in Great Britain by Cox and Wyman Ltd

About this Book

Like many people I was familiar with the latest "hi-tech" uses of the Internet - webcams, e-mail, booking holidays, buying and selling on eBay, etc., etc. However, until recently, I did not fully appreciate the amount of high quality help and support the Internet can provide on many of the most important and serious problems in life, especially those affecting older people.

Early chapters of this book explain methods of connecting to the Internet, including accessibility features to help those with special needs such as limited vision and mobility. The book then describes the basic methods of navigating the Web, bookmarking favourite sites and printing information.

The Adobe Acrobat PDF format is the standard medium for sending official Government and business documents over the Internet. Adobe documents are described in detail, including downloading the free Adobe Acrobat Reader.

After explaining the basic methods of searching for information, the book shows how to find help on topics concerning many older people. These include pensions and benefits, savings and investments, housing options and equity release, as well as diet, health and fitness. Another chapter covers the legal issues facing older people such as wills, inheritance tax and funerals, etc. Help in finding special equipment, home adaptations and support for elderly and disabled people is also covered. The Internet is particularly valuable for anyone with restricted mobility, since all sorts of information and official documents can be viewed and printed in the comfort of your own home.

As a member of the older generation myself, I have personal experience of many of the topics in this book. This book is part of the very successful "Older Generation" series from Bernard Babani (publishing) Ltd.

About the Author

Jim Gatenby trained as a Chartered Mechanical Engineer and initially worked at Rolls-Royce Ltd using computers in the analysis of jet engine performance. He obtained a Master of Philosophy degree in Mathematical Education by research at Loughborough University of Technology and taught mathematics and computing to 'A' Level for many years. His most recent posts included Head of Computer Studies and Information Technology Coordinator. During this time he has written many books in the fields of educational computing and Microsoft Windows.

The author, himself a member of the over 50s club, has considerable experience of teaching students in school and adult education on GCSE Computing and Computer Literacy and Information Technology (CLAIT) courses.

Trademarks

Microsoft, MSN, Microsoft Word, Windows, Windows Explorer, Windows Update and Windows XP are either trademarks or registered trademarks of Microsoft Corporation. F-Secure, Virus Protection and Internet Shield are either trademarks or registered trademarks of F-Secure Corporation. Norton AntiVirus is a trademark of Symantec Corporation. McAfee VirusScan is a registered trademark of McAfee, Inc. Adobe Acrobat is a trademark of Adobe Systems Incorporated. Google is a trademark of Google, Inc. Yahoo! is a trademark or registered trademark of Yahoo!, Inc. Ask Jeeves and Excite are registered trademarks of Ask Jeeves, Inc. AltaVista is a trademark of Overture Services, Inc. Lycos ® is a registered trademark of Carnegie Mellon University.

All other brand and product names used in this book are recognized as trademarks or registered trademarks, of their respective companies.

Acknowledgements

The author and publishers would like to thank the following businesses and organizations for allowing extracts from their Web sites to be published in this book:

1Stop Finance, Alcohol Concern, ATOC, Barton Hill Advice Service, CenNet, Diet-i.com, Directgov, EQUIP-NHS, Excite.co.uk, Find a Property, Google Inc., Greenwich Council, HBOS plc, IndependentAge, Later Life Training Ltd, Laterlife.com Limited, Lawpack Publishing Ltd, Leicestershire County Council, Leonard Cheshire, MoneyExpert, Moneyextra, MYFINANCES.CO.UK, National Express Ltd, Netdoctor.co.uk, NHS Direct, Nottingham City Council, RDK Mobility, Silver Surfers, Sixtyplusurfers, Tax Café, The Association of Retired and Persons Over 50 (ARP050), The British Nutrition Foundation, The Court Service, The Deafblind Manual Alphabet, The Department for Work and Pensions, The Disabled Living Centres Council, The Financial Services Authority, The Motley Fool, The National Heart, Lung and Blood Institute (US), The Pension Service, The Pensions Advisory Service, This Is Money, WeightWatchers.co.uk Limited, Wildblueberries.com.

I would also like to thank my son, David Gatenby, for his help in the research for this book.

Viewing the Latest Web Pages

The Web sites included in this book are used as examples to illustrate the text and are current at the time of writing. However, Web pages may be amended or updated from time to time; for example to change prices or to include special offers.

Similarly pensions, benefits, allowances and taxes, etc., may be changed by the Chancellor in the Budget, usually with effect from the following April.

Therefore readers requiring any sort of factual information are advised to view the latest Web pages on a computer connected to the Internet. The addresses of the Web sites featured in this book are given throughout the text, for example:

www.moneyexpert.com

Simply enter the relevant address into the address bar of a browser (such as Internet Explorer) to view the latest version of the Web pages and get the most up-to-date information.

IMPORTANT NOTICE

The information given in this book is intended for illustrative purposes only, to demonstrate the way the Internet can be used to find information on a wide range of subjects. This should help the reader to acquire a great deal of useful factual knowledge and information. However, anyone worried about a specific problem **should always consult an appropriately qualified professional in the relevant field, such as a doctor, lawyer or financial adviser.**

Contents

4

5

6

1

Getting Started

Introduction

Being a member of the "older generation" myself I have worked with computers and the Internet for many years. For some of us it was necessary to acquire computing skills in order to adapt to a changing working environment.

Many older people have asked "What use are computers and the Internet to me?" – seeing the new technology as the exclusive preserve of the young, with their enthusiasm for the latest games or downloading music and videos. In fact, as people get older and less mobile, the Internet becomes increasingly valuable as a source of help and information.

The Internet has developed over the years into something much broader and more accessible than a "gee-whiz" high-tech marvel. Recently my wife and I have been overtaken by the sort of events which affect many of us in later life – serious illness, looking after older relatives, bereavement, etc. In addition, the meltdown in some pension funds and share prices has caused many of us to look hard at ways of surviving financially in retirement.

We have been amazed at the way the Internet can deliver high quality advice and information on literally any aspect of life for older people – and all immediately available in the comfort of your own home.

An Ageing Population

With ever more people now living to a ripe old age, (there are currently over 11 million pensioners in Britain), there is an increasing need for good advice on a wide range of issues particularly relevant to the older generation. At the time of writing many older people have seen their pensions and investments slump in value – far below their previous expectations.

Many people are not aware of the substantial benefits to which they may be legally entitled and so millions of pounds go unclaimed each year. In 2003 it was reported that £2bn (£2,000,000,000) of available benefits such as Minimum Income Guarantee, Council Tax Benefit and Housing Benefit went unclaimed. The money is there for collection but the message is just not getting through.

Apart from approximately 2 million pensioners in low-income households, pensioners with substantial savings may also be eligible for some financial help.

One of the problems is that many older people don't receive vital information about their entitlements. Or they may receive leaflets which are difficult to read and forms which are too complicated to fill in. However, thanks to the Internet, a great deal of good quality help and advice is now available easily and quickly.

Some older people may not have the facilities or the skills to access the Internet on their own; it is hoped that this book will also help younger family members and carers to obtain advice for older people from the Internet.

What is the Scope of the Internet?

I have never failed to find useful Web pages on any subject no matter how bizarre. In the context of this book there is copious advice for older people, on topics such as:

- Pensions and benefits
- Healthy living
- Finding out about illnesses
- Savings and investments
- Obtaining help and support for elderly and disabled people
- Maintaining and adapting a home
- Releasing some of the equity in a home
- Alternative housing options in later life
- Wills, executors and inheritance tax
- Registering a death and arranging a funeral
- Obtaining probate and administering an estate.

Of course, some of the topics listed above involve life-changing events. This book does not suggest for one moment that the Internet should be used as an alternative to the advice of qualified professionals. For example, in matters such as serious illness or legal issues you should always consult a doctor or solicitor, etc. However, there is enough good quality advice available on the Internet to enable anyone to become conversant with virtually any topic which concerns them. This may lead to the solution of a worrying problem; alternatively it may help you to prepare yourself thoroughly before meeting a professional adviser – after all, forewarned is forearmed.

What is the Quality of the Information on the Internet?

If you listen to reports in the media you could be forgiven for thinking that the Internet is only used for pornography or sophisticated crime. I know of at least one person who totally ignores the Internet for this reason. In fact, as this book will show, most of the information is provided by a wide range of ethical organizations and institutions and stored on millions of computers around the world. The information providers include:

- Universities and research organizations
- Professional bodies and learned societies
- Charities and other not-for-profit organizations
- Large multi-national corporations
- Private companies
- Commercial Web sites giving news and advice
- Government departments such as the NHS
- Local authorities, county councils, etc.

There are quite a few Web sites provided especially to help older people with news, special offers and general advice and information about most aspects of later life. These often provide *online forums* in which you can discuss topics which interest you. You type in your "conversation" and exchange views with people all round the world.

Some Web sites appear to exist purely to give advice but actually make money from the advertisements around the edge of their Web pages. Then there are Web sites which give a "taste" of introductory advice about a subject in the hope of signing you up for a paid service such as financial or legal advice. As with any purchase or transaction, it's a case of *caveat emptor* – let the buyer beware.

Advantages of Getting Advice from the Internet

- The computer and Internet connection sitting in your home will provide advice on a wide range of subjects – legal, financial, health, etc. There's no need to get on a bus or drive a car to the post office or council offices, etc., and no need to stand in a queue or make frustrating telephone calls. This convenience may be especially welcome if you need advice during distressing times such as bereavement or if you are disabled.

- Advice from the Internet is immediate – you don't need to wait for an appointment with an adviser.

- If you're looking for information on an aspect of health, for example, you can read information contributed by a large number of experts – not just the one who happens to be near your home.

- There's no need to order documents and application forms and wait for them to arrive in the post. You can download and print official booklets and in some cases fill in forms on the screen.

- Web pages displaying useful information can be printed on paper and kept for future reference.

- The advice you get from the Internet should be up-to-date – it's just a case of the information provider changing the Web page on their *host computer*.

- Advice from the Internet is usually free (apart from the cost of your computer and Internet connection). Professional experts, with their office overheads, etc., may charge you for similar advice given during a face-to-face consultation.

What Equipment is Needed?

The Computer

Most computers sold in the High Street are known as *PCs*, after the original IBM Personal Computer. In fact there are thousands of manufacturers and assemblers building PCs. Most of these machines use the Microsoft Windows operating system, which controls the screen display and the overall operation of the computer. This is achieved through a system of windows, i.e. rectangular areas and icons (small pictures) on the screen, selected by a mouse.

The PC has become the world-wide standard for home and business computers and has generated a huge amount of software, i.e. programs. There is also plenty of support for the PC, including spare parts and people experienced in carrying out repairs and upgrades to incorporate new developments in technology.

Nowadays the only serious alternative to the PC computer is the Apple Macintosh, in various forms. The Apple Mac has many devoted users since it was the pioneer of easy-to-use mouse and windows operating systems. The Mac has established itself as the preferred choice in many printing and publishing enterprises and in areas of education.

For the general user, however, who wishes to remain in the mainstream of readily-available software, hardware and support, there isn't much choice other than to buy a PC machine running Microsoft Windows.

You will also need to obtain a device called a *modem* to connect your computer to the Internet via a telephone socket in your home. (This socket can be provided by one of the cheap adapters available in most DIY stores).

Choosing a Supplier

When buying a computer system, you may choose to visit one of the large retailers who put together some very attractive packages, often including a free printer and modem. Alternatively you might purchase a computer from one of the many small one or two-person companies who build their own computers for as little as £500 including VAT. These will often build a computer to the customer's own specification to include a faster *processor*, or more *memory* or a bigger *hard disc drive* than standard. (For help with this jargon, please see the note at the bottom of this page).

If possible, try to find a business that is recommended by satisfied customers. With the small supplier you can go back to the person who built your computer if there are any problems. In the case of the large supplier or mail order company, your machine may need to be sent away for repair for several weeks. Fortunately modern computers are very reliable and you will probably have no problems.

Plan for the Future

If you buy a new computer system it will definitely be powerful enough to cope with finding information from the Internet. However, computers become out of date after a few years, because of developments in technology, so it's a good idea to buy the most powerful machine you can afford.

Please note:

More details of computers and the functions of their various components are given in one of my earlier books:

Computing for the Older Generation

Bernard Babani (publishing) Ltd

Connecting to the Internet

In order to connect to the Internet you need:

- A computer and preferably a printer
- A modem and cables
- A telephone socket
- A connection to an Internet Service Provider (ISP).

The modem is a small electronic circuit board which is usually connected with cables between your computer and the telephone socket. It is used to enable the *digital* data from the computer to be transmitted and received along the telephone lines, which work with *audio* data. You can either have an *external* modem which is enclosed in a box and is designed to sit on your desk or an *internal* modem which plugs inside of your computer. The external modem has diagnostic lights on the outside, giving you information about what it's doing.

Broadband versus 56K Modem

The main choice with modems is between the traditional *56K modem* and the later *broadband system*. Without going into too much jargon, 56K refers to the *nominal* speed with which the modem transmits and receives data. Both systems work by connecting through the standard telephone network to a computer server, i.e. host computer, provided by an Internet Service Provider (ISP). These include companies such as AOL, Tiscali and the Microsoft Network (MSN) for example. You pay a subscription to the ISP, who in return provides you with news, information (and advertisements), e-mail facilities and acts as a gateway to connect your computer to the millions of other computers on the Internet.

Until recently many areas of Britain were not able to access a broadband service because modifications were needed to local telephone exchanges. This situation has improved significantly at the time of writing.

The broadband system is expensive (costing about £17-£30 per month) but is recommended for the following reasons:

- Broadband is up to 10 times the speed of the 56K modem, enabling you to find information faster.

- An ordinary telephone and broadband Internet can be used at the same time, unlike the 56K system.

- The broadband connection is usually left on all day – you don't need to keep "dialling up".

However, if you can't afford the more expensive broadband system, a 56K modem will be quite adequate for the sort of tasks outlined in this book – they'll just take a little longer. Typical charges for the 56K dial-up service range from a pay-as-you go service with no monthly charges to an unlimited access service (with no additional call charges) costing £15 a month.

The 56K modem connects straight into an ordinary telephone socket. The broadband connection requires a special ADSL modem. You also need a small splitter device known as a *filter* to enable the broadband Internet and an ordinary telephone to be used at the same time. Making the connection to an Internet Service Provider is usually just a case of inserting a free CD and following the instructions on the screen. The CDs are often supplied with computing magazines or available to be picked up from supermarkets. Alternatively, any good computer shop or freelance computer builder/repairer will set up your Internet connection in a matter of minutes.

Sharing an Internet Connection Between Computers

If you have more than one computer in your house, you may want to consider *networking*. In the past this has meant joining computers together with cables so that they could all use the same Internet connection or share devices such as printers. You can also send messages between networked computers and share files of information. For some years I connected my "home office" computer to the family machine using the traditional cable method, known as Ethernet. This works well but can involve drilling through walls and running cables around your home. Next I used a BT system which allows you to connect computers using ordinary telephone extension cables around the house.

Currently I am changing to a *wireless* or *WiFi* network. This allows you to connect computers using radio signals; there is no need for any cables between the special modem and the various computers. A networking device known as a *router* is needed in addition to an ADSL broadband modem. Combined units incorporating both an ADSL modem and a router are also available. It is possible to have a wireless network consisting of a mixture of "desktop" and "laptop" computers. This means, for example, you could take a laptop computer and use it anywhere in your home; you could even surf the Internet while sitting in your garden on a summer's day.

Please Note:

The process of connecting to the Internet is covered in more detail in one of my earlier books:

The Internet for the Older Generation

Bernard Babani (publishing) Ltd

Microsoft Windows

This is the name of the software used to "drive" your computer. If you buy a new computer it is likely to have Microsoft Windows XP already installed. If you have an older machine it may have an earlier version of the software such as Windows 95, 98 or Windows Me. In order to keep up with the latest developments it's a good idea to make sure you've got a recent version such as Windows XP Home Edition. If you have an elderly computer, the bad news is that it may not be powerful enough to run Windows XP. If in doubt, consult a local computer shop, etc.

Windows XP (and the earlier versions of Windows) are known as *operating systems*. Windows XP controls the screen display and the windows, icons and menus which allow you to start programs and perform operations such as saving and printing your work on paper.

When you first start your computer, the screen displays the Windows Desktop. This includes a number of icons or small pictures representing different programs, files or links to Internet Web sites. These icons are known as *shortcuts*; they allow you to perform an operation by simply double-clicking the mouse without having to go through a series of menus. You can place any number of icons on the Windows Desktop as shortcuts to the programs, folders and Web sites that you use frequently.

Windows XP also includes the Web browser software, Internet Explorer, which allows you to find, navigate and manage Web pages, as discussed in Chapter 3.

The *start* menu in Windows XP gives access to all of the programs on your computer. It is launched by clicking the *start* button at the bottom left of the screen as shown below.

Programs are launched after clicking the **All Programs** button. Windows XP features such as the **Control Panel** and **Printers and Faxes** are used to set up and manage the software and hardware devices on the computer.

Launching a Program in Microsoft Windows

As mentioned earlier, a program can be often be started by double-clicking an icon on the Windows Desktop. Frequently used programs such as **Internet Explorer, Microsoft Outlook** and **Microsoft Word** are also represented automatically by icons in the left-hand panel of the *start* menu as shown on the previous page. A single click on any of these icons launches the program.

If there is no icon for a program then you can launch it by clicking its name in the **All Programs** feature on the *start* menu, as shown below and on the previous page.

To create an icon for a program on the Windows Desktop, right-click the program's name in the *start*, **All Programs** menu as shown above. This invokes the menu shown below, from which you select **Desktop (create shortcut)**. This puts an icon for the program on the Windows Desktop. Double-click the icon to start the program.

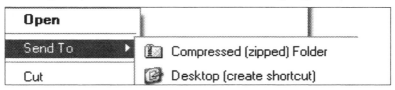

Microsoft Windows is covered in more detail in one of my earlier books:

Computing for the Older Generation

Bernard Babani (publishing) Ltd

Protecting Your Computer

Connecting a computer to the Internet can make it vulnerable to attack from outside. The main dangers are:

Viruses

A virus is a small program designed maliciously to spread around the Internet and cause damage and inconvenience. Files sent across the Internet as *attachments* to e-mail messages are a common source of viruses.

Your computer can be protected against viruses by the installation of inexpensive anti-virus software such as Norton AntiVirus, McAfee VirusScan and F-Secure. These packages can save a great deal of time, expense and inconvenience. Some anti-virus software can be "downloaded" from the Internet and used free for a while.

New viruses are being created all the time, so you need to keep up-to-date by downloading new versions of the anti-virus software from the Internet, usually for a subscription.

Computer Crime

Determined "hackers" can read financial information such as credit card details from a vulnerable computer connected to the Internet. A program called a *firewall* detects other computers trying to connect to yours and prevents access. Companies such as Norton, Sygate, eTrust EZ and McAfee all provide inexpensive firewall software. Some integrated packages include both firewalls and anti-virus software.

Updates to Microsoft Windows XP

The **Windows Update** feature allows you to download and install on your computer the latest security modifications to Windows XP. Windows Update should be used regularly.

Help for Users With Special Needs

Introduction

Microsoft Windows XP contains a number of features to help users with impairments in any of the following:

- Vision
- Hearing
- Mobility.

The special needs features in Windows XP are fairly basic and some users with special needs may require more specialised accessibility software. However, the tools included in Windows XP are free and should help some users with special needs to get more out of their computer and the Internet. The features are launched by selecting **start**, **All Programs**, **Accessories** and **Accessibility**.

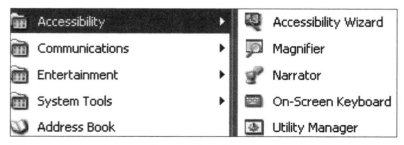

The next section looks at the five **Accessibility** options, shown in the right-hand panel above.

The Accessibility Wizard

A wizard is a program which leads you through a series of interactive screens. The user makes selections from various choices before clicking **Next** to move on to the next screen. Wizards are frequently used in Microsoft Windows for setting up new hardware and software.

Start the **Accessibility Wizard** by clicking *start*, **All Programs, Accessories** and **Accessibility**. First you see the **Accessibility Welcome Screen** and on clicking **Next** you are given the option to select a larger text size.

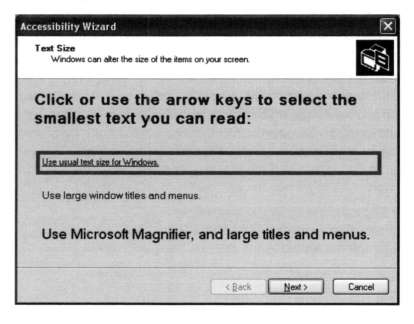

Further dialogue boxes in the wizard allow you to increase the text size which appears in window title bars and also to increase the size of scroll bars.

Then you are asked to specify your own special needs, by ticking the check boxes for conditions which apply to you.

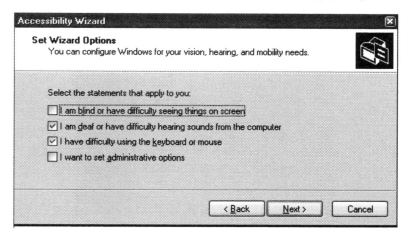

The Accessibility Wizard then proceeds in one of several ways, depending on the ticks you have placed in the above check boxes. For example, if your vision is impaired, the option to display large icons is presented, as shown below.

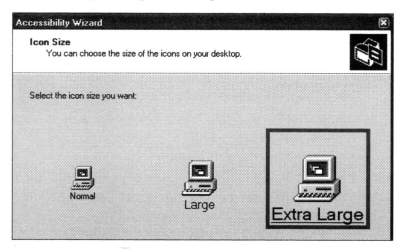

Another dialogue box allows you to select a high-contrast colour display and this is followed by a box giving a choice of various colours and sizes of *mouse cursor*.

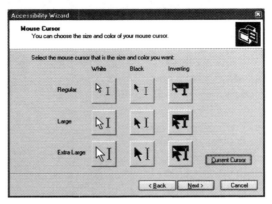

If you have difficulty using a mouse, the numeric keypad on the right of the keyboard can be used instead. For example, the cursor can be controlled by the arrow keys, a mouse-click is replaced by pressing the number **5** key and double-clicking is replaced by the + key. Finally a dialogue box appears allowing you to swap the function of the left and right mouse buttons, to work with your preferred hand.

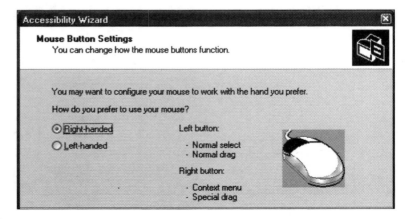

After completing all of the dialogue boxes, click **Finish** to leave the Accessibility Wizard. Please note that you can also set the **Accessibility Options** without using the Wizard. First enter the **Control Panel** from the *start* menu. Make sure the **Control Panel** is in **Classic View**. If the **Control Panel** is currently in **Category View**, click **Switch to Classic View** from the top left-hand corner of the **Control Panel**.

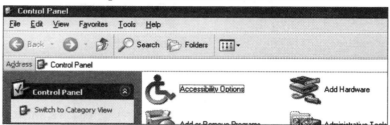

Now double-click the icon for **Accessibility Options**. The following dialogue box opens. A series of tabs (**Keyboard, Sound, Display,** etc.) give access to many further options.

The Magnifier

This feature enables the person with impaired vision to enlarge different areas of the screen, as required. The Magnifier is started by clicking *start*, **All Programs**, **Accessories**, **Accessibility** and **Magnifier**, as shown below.

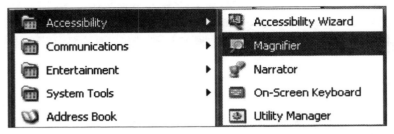

A settings dialogue box also appears, giving you the option to change the magnification level in the range 1 to 9.

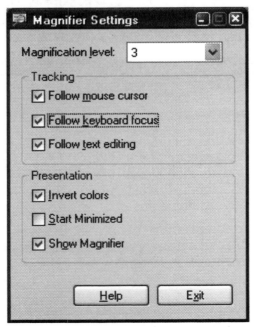

You are presented with a note stating that the Magnifier is intended for users with slight visual impairment. Those with more serious visual problems may need a program with higher functionality.

Note in the dialogue box on the previous page, you can set the magnifier to follow the mouse cursor and the keyboard focus. You can also invert colours to make the screen easier to read. The magnifier appears in its own window above the normal screen. As you move about the normal screen, the magnifier tracks the cursor or keyboard and displays the local text and graphics enlarged, as if viewed through a magnifying glass. Shown below is a screenshot from Microsoft Internet Explorer, with the magnifier running. The area of the screen around the current position is shown magnified across the top of the screen.

The Narrator

If your computer is fitted with a sound card and speakers, the Narrator can read out the text in menus and describe features such as buttons in dialogue boxes. The Narrator can also read out the letters and keys pressed as you type them into a document. To start the program, select **start**, **All Programs**, **Accessories**, **Accessibility** and **Narrator**.

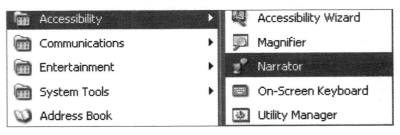

After clicking **Narrator**, an introductory window appears informing you that **Narrator** only works in English and may not work well with certain software. The user is also referred to the Microsoft Web site for details of other "screen reader" software. After clicking **OK** a dialogue box appears allowing the various options to be set in Narrator.

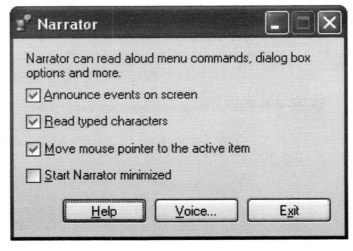

The On-Screen Keyboard

This feature is intended for anyone with mobility problems, who finds it difficult to handle a normal keyboard. The **On-Screen Keyboard** is launched from *start*, **All Programs**, **Accessories**, **Accessibility** and **On-Screen Keyboard**.

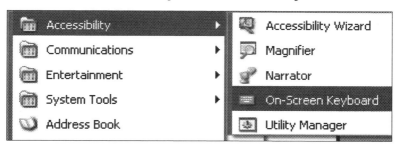

The on-screen keyboard is operated by a mouse or perhaps another type of pointing device. The cursor is moved over the required letter and the mouse is clicked, causing the letter to appear on the page at the current cursor position.

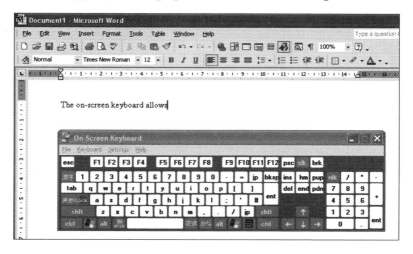

The Utility Manager

The **Utility Manager** is started from *start*, **All Programs**, **Accessories**, **Accessibility** and **Utility Manager**.

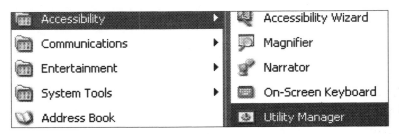

A dialogue box appears showing, within a single window, the special needs programs which are currently running. Here the programs can be started, stopped or configured.

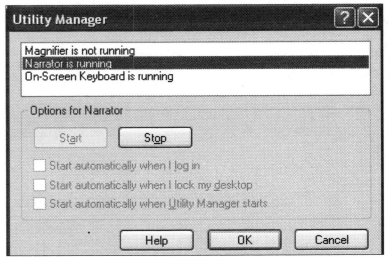

The previous pages describe the special needs features provided free within Windows XP. The Microsoft Web site gives details of additional specialist software and hardware resources to help users with a range of impairments.

Navigating Web Sites

Introduction

A *browser* is a program used to view Web pages. When you connect to the Internet you are normally directed to the *home page* of your Internet Service Provider, displayed in your browser. From here you can branch to other Web pages, either by clicking on special *links* or by entering the *address* of another Web page. The browser also allows you to *search* for pages containing certain information. Microsoft Windows includes its own browser, Internet Explorer, which appears on the *start* menu, shown below.

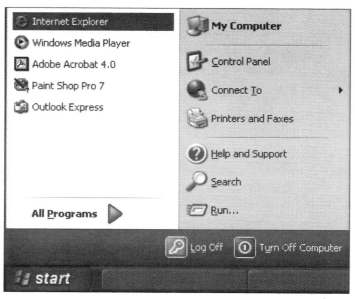

3 Navigating Web Sites

This chapter is based on the Internet Explorer Web browser, but there are other alternatives such as Netscape Navigator. To launch the browser, click **start**, then **Internet Explorer**, as shown on the previous page. Alternatively click the **Internet Explorer** icon on the Windows Desktop as shown on the right.

The computer should connect to the Internet and display the home page of your Internet Service Provider. However, it's possible to set your computer to start up and display a different home page of your own and this is discussed later.

In the main body of the MSN home page shown above are various news items; around the Web page are various advertisements which can be clicked to yield more information.

Clickable Links

As you move the cursor about a Web page you will notice that the cursor sometimes changes from an arrow to a hand. When this happens over a piece of text, the text changes colour and is also underlined, as shown on the MSN **Money** page on the left. A small rectangular caption also appears showing the name of the topic highlighted. Whenever the hand appears on the screen, this means the cursor is over a clickable *link* (or *hyperlink)* to another Web page. Pictures are also used as links to other Web pages. Links allow you to move from page to page on the Internet, between different pages on the current Web site. Alternatively a link may lead to pages on a totally different Web site stored on a computer on the other side of the world.

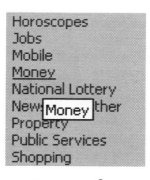

When you click the **Money** link as shown above, the MSN **Money** page opens up as shown on the next page.

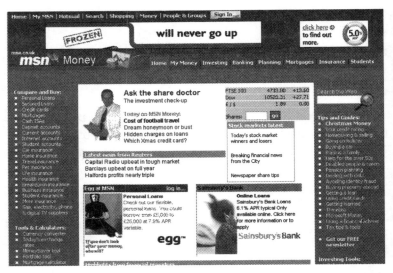

The Web page above includes lots of further links which become apparent when you move the pointer around the screen. Again the pointer changes to a hand and the text of the link changes colour and is underlined. In the above example, the pictures also act as links to other Web pages.

Down the right-hand side of the MSN Money Web page shown above, under **Tips and Guides:** is a further set of links as shown in the extract on the right. These include **Help for the over 50s, Disabled people & carers** and **Pension planning**. Click on any of these links to see notes on each subject and also further links to the Web sites of relevant Government departments and other information providers.

Tips and Guides:
- **Christmas Money**
- Your credit rating
- Homebuying & selling
- Going on holiday
- Buying a car
- Raising a family
- Help for the over 50s
- Disabled people & carers
- Pension planning

The Toolbar

After you have moved between several pages, you may want to retrace your steps at some point. The Toolbar across the top of Internet Explorer has a number of icons which help you to "surf the Net".

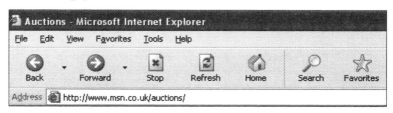

For example, as shown above, there are buttons to move **Forward** and **Back** through previously visited Web pages.

The **Stop** button shown above is used when a Web page is taking too long to load and you suspect a fault.

If a message appears saying a Web page cannot be displayed, try clicking the **Refresh** button on the Toolbar, as shown above and on the right. You can also click **Refresh** to make sure your browser is displaying the latest version of a Web page, since some pages are updated from time to time.

Towards the middle of the Toolbar there is the **Home** icon to return you to your home page. Three more icons towards the right of the Toolbar can be used to search for information and to revisit Web pages that you have already viewed.

These are **Search**, **Favorites**, and **History** shown right. These features are discussed in more detail shortly.

Using the Address Bar to Connect to a Web Site

To use this method of finding a Web site, you obviously need to obtain the address first, perhaps from an advertisement, newspaper article or radio or television program. Every Web site has a unique address, such as **http://www.thisismoney.co.uk/**. This is typed into the **Address** bar of the Web browser, as shown below.

In computing jargon, the address of a Web site is known as a *URL* or *Uniform Resource Locator*. In the above example, the meanings of the parts of the address are as follows:

http:

HyperText Transfer Protocol. This is a set of rules used by Web servers. **ftp** is another protocol used for transferring files across the Internet.

www

This means the site is part of the World Wide Web.

thisismoney

This is the name of the company or organization hosting the Web site on its server computer.

co

This denotes a Web site owned by a UK company.

Other common *domains* (as these address extensions are known) include:

com   Company or Commercial organisation

edu   Education

org   Non-profit making organization

gov   Government

net   Internet company

If you know the address of a Web site, enter this into the address bar at the top of the Web browser as shown below. (In practice you can miss out the **http://** part of the address.)

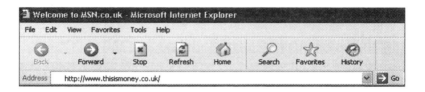

When you click the **Go** button or press **Enter** your browser should connect to the  Web site and display its home page on the screen. Then you can start moving about the site using the links within the page as described earlier. If you click the downward pointing arrowhead to the left of the **Go** button shown above, a drop-down menu appears with a list of the addresses of your recently visited Web sites. If you click one of the addresses it will be placed in the **Address** bar and you can then connect to that Web site by clicking **Go**.

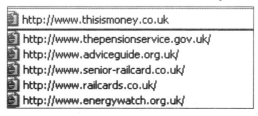

Revisiting Web Sites - Favorites or Bookmarks

If you find a Web site which you think may be useful in future, a link to the site can be saved after clicking the **Favorites** icon on the Toolbar in Internet Explorer.

Favorites save you the task of typing what may be a lengthy URL (www...., etc.,) into the **Address** bar. After you select **Favorites**, a panel opens on the left of the screen, displaying a list of Web sites, as shown below.

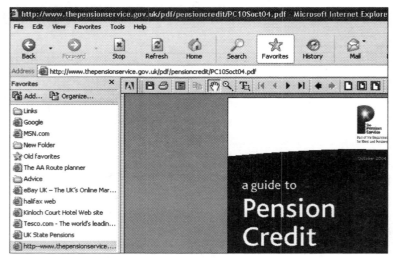

© Crown Copyright

Click on the required **Favorite** to connect to and open up the Web page. In this example a page from the Pension Service Web site has been stored as a **Favorite** then opened.

To save a Web site on your list of **Favorites** click the **Add...** button in the **Favorites** panel. First make sure your browser is currently displaying the required Web page. In this case I shall be adding the

Pension Service Home Page to my list of **Favorites**. A dialogue box opens up as shown below.

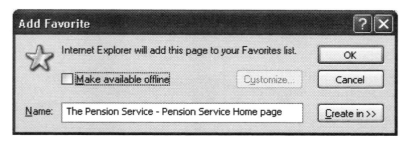

Note in the **Add Favorite** dialogue box above, you can insert a name of your own if you wish. Click **OK** to add the site to your **Favorites** list. Clicking the **Create in** button shown above enables you to create the new **Favorite** in a folder of your choice.

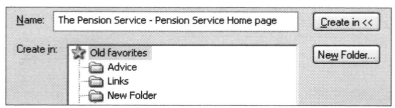

The **Organize...** option shown at the top right of this page allows you to create folders and move, delete and rename **Favorites**.

3 Navigating Web Sites

After you have added a Web site to your **Favorites** list, to return to the Web site at a later date, click the **Favorites** icon, then click the name of the Web site in the list.

In this example, the Pension Service Web site opens on the screen, as shown below.

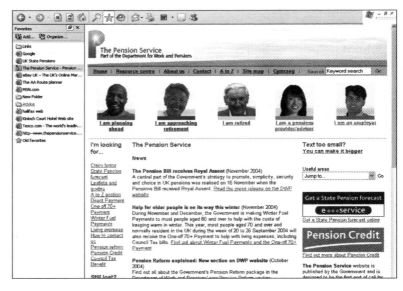

© Crown Copyright

The History Feature

The **History** feature is a list of links to the Web sites you have visited in recent days. As discussed later in this chapter, you can set the number of days for which links are kept. To have a look at your **History** list click the icon on the right of the Internet Explorer Toolbar shown right and below.

The History feature opens up in a panel on the left of the screen as shown below.

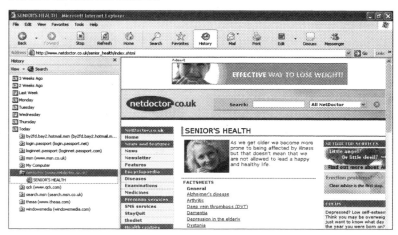

Click on a day to reveal the links for that day as shown on the right. Then click a link to return to a particular site.

Housekeeping Tasks in Internet Explorer

As mentioned earlier you can set the number of days to keep links in the **History** feature. From the menu bar along the top of Internet Explorer, select **Tools** and **Internet Options....** The **Internet Options** dialogue box opens up with the **General** tab selected, as shown below.

At the bottom of the **Internet Options** dialogue box shown previously is a small box for setting the number of days to keep links in the **History** feature. As shown below there is also a button to clear the entries in the **History** feature.

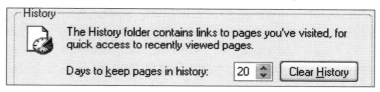

At the top of the **Internet Options** dialogue box shown on the previous page is a box which allows you to change your **Home page**. As mentioned earlier, this is the page which your browser normally opens on connection to the Internet.

To change your **Home page**, type a new entry in the **Address:** bar as shown above.

While working on the Internet, a lot of *temporary files* are saved on your hard disc. These can be safely removed using the **Delete Cookies...** and **Delete Files...** buttons shown below, which appear in the middle of the **Internet Options** dialogue box shown on the previous page.

Creating a Shortcut to a Web Site

If you find a Web site that you are likely to return to regularly, you can place a *shortcut icon* on the Windows Desktop. (The Desktop is the screen which appears when you first start up the computer). Then, whenever you want to connect to the site, you simply double-click its icon on the Windows Desktop. For example, suppose you want to return regularly to the Web site **This is Money**.

www.thisismoney.co.uk

With the Web page displayed on the screen, *right-click* over the page, (but not over a picture). From the menu which appears select the **Create Shortcut** option. This places an icon for the Web site on the Windows Desktop. *Double-click* this icon whenever you want to return directly to the **This is Money** Web site.

Printing a Web Page

When computers first arrived in business it was thought that paper would become a thing of the past – the "paperless office" would reign supreme. In fact, if anything, the reverse is probably true; we may be using more paper than ever before. This is certainly the case if the stacks of paper marked "Laser" and "Inkjet" in stationery shops are any indication.

In fact it's very often useful to be able to print a Web page out on paper (known as "hard copy" in the computing jargon). For example, you might want to give a copy of some information to someone who doesn't have a computer. Or you might be involved in meetings and discussions away from the computer or be compiling a dossier of information on a subject close to your heart.

Internet Explorer has an option to print Web pages. From the menu select **File** and **Print...**. Or use the **Print** icon on the Internet Explorer Toolbar. It's a good idea to use the **Print Preview...** option shown on the right before trying to print a Web page. This shows how the page will appear on paper.

Also watch out for links which sometimes appear on a Web page allowing you to select a **Printer Friendly Version** of the page. Click this link and then select **File** and **Print**.

Searching Within a Web Site

Searching the entire Internet for information requires a special program called a *search engine*. The most well-known search engine at the time of writing is Google and this topic is covered in detail in Chapter 5. However, many Web sites have their own built-in search facility, so that the search is confined only to the narrow content of the particular Web site. For example, **The Motley Fool** financial Web site has its own search bar as shown below, allowing you to find lots of articles on a particular subject.

www.fool.co.uk

For example, entering **over 50s** in the **Search** bar and clicking **Go** as shown above, produces a list of links to relevant articles, all from within the Motley Fool Web site.

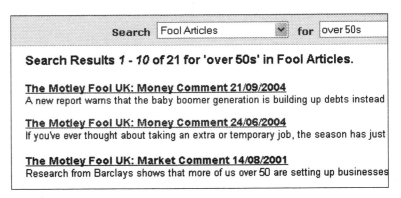

Obtaining Documents from the Internet

Introduction

The Internet is a source of thousands of useful documents which can be "downloaded" to your computer, such as official booklets containing essential information on health, pensions and personal finance. You can view them on the screen or print them on paper using a program called Adobe Reader. This can all be achieved on your own computer in the comfort of your own home. The alternative is to wait days while a copy of the booklet is posted to you or you have to travel to the nearest post office or tax office to pick up a copy.

This chapter explains how to obtain a free copy of Adobe Reader and use it to read and print documents.

PDF Files

Documents intended for downloading from the Internet are usually in a special format known as PDF (or Portable Document Format). Adobe Acrobat, a relative of Adobe Reader, allows you to take any file, such as a document saved in Microsoft Word or Excel, and convert it to the PDF format. The original fonts (i.e. styles of lettering) and the pictures and layout are all accurately preserved in the new PDF file.

Anyone with a copy of the freely available Adobe Reader program can view and print all sorts of documents in the PDF format, regardless of the computer systems and software used to create them originally.

As an example, this book was originally typed on a PC computer using Microsoft Word. Then it was converted to PDF format using Adobe Acrobat. The resulting files can then be read accurately on any type of computer system, such as the Apple Macintosh favoured by many printing and publishing companies.

If you want to create your own PDF then you need to purchase the full Adobe Acrobat program.

Installing Adobe Reader on Your Computer

If your computer does not already have a copy of Adobe Reader stored on its hard disc, you can easily get one after logging on to the Adobe Web site as shown below.

www.adobe.co.uk

The panel shown here on the right appears on the left-hand side of the Adobe opening page. If you click the link **Adobe PDF will change the way you package your work** you can learn more about the program and watch an Adobe PDF TV commercial.

To start the process of obtaining a free copy of the program, click the link **Get Adobe Reader** shown on the right. (Please note that many of the Web sites distributing documents in PDF format also include the link **Get Adobe Reader** shown above on the right.)

You then complete the dialogue box shown below.

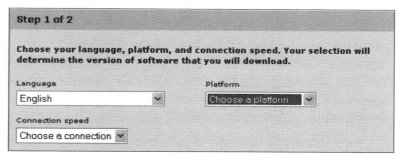

This includes selecting your **Platform** from a menu (shown right) which pops-up when you click the arrow next to **Choose a platform** (shown above). The platform is your operating system such as Windows XP, Windows 98, MacOS, etc. (A small sample of the available platforms is shown in the extract on the right).

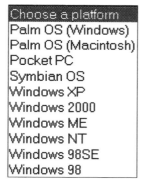

After choosing your **Language** the **Connection speed** must be selected from either **dial-up** or **broadband**. If you are not sure about the connection speed, dial-up uses the older, slower

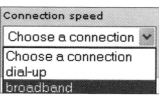

traditional modem. Broadband is the new, much faster Internet connection which is always online. Broadband has not been accessible for very long in certain parts of Britain; if your system has been installed for more than a couple of years it most probably uses a dial-up modem.

After completing the previous dialogue box scroll down the Adobe Web page where you can read more about the download process. There are tick boxes to select which software to download including Adobe Reader and also a free copy of Adobe Photoshop Album 2.0 Starter Edition. You are also advised to download the optional **Adobe Download Manager** which assists in the process of downloading and installing Adobe software.

Step 2 of 2

Download file size: 22.4MB
Download file: Adobe Reader 6.0.1, and Photoshop Album Starter Edition 2.0.1

☑ Download the full version of Adobe Reader (recommended), allowing me to:

- Search PDF files
- Activate accessibility features built into PDF files
- View Adobe Photoshop Album slide shows and electronic cards, extract pictures, and order prints
- Play back embedded movies, animation, and sound
- View, organize, and purchase eBooks

After reading notes on how to obtain **Updates** to the version of Adobe Reader, click **Continue** to display the **download** button shown below.

 Adobe   Products   Solutions   Support

Adobe Reader

Download your copy of Adobe® Reader® software.

 download

Thank you!

When you click **download** as shown on the previous page, the following dialogue box appears, giving the choice of running or saving the **Adobe Download Manager**.

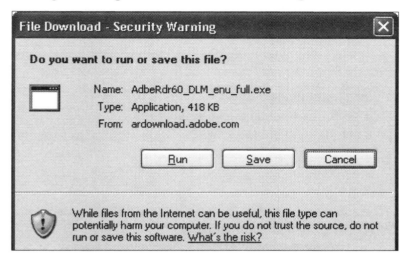

Before proceeding with the **Run** and **Save** options above it is worth reading the notes at the bottom of the box and clicking **What's the risk?** – a warning about viruses.

The subject of virus checking is covered in more detail in our very popular companion book "Computing for the Older Generation" from Bernard Babani (publishing) Ltd.

If you know that your computer has up-to-date virus protection, click either **Run** to start the Adobe Download Manager directly or **Save** to place a copy of the program on your hard disc. The **Save As** dialogue box then appears enabling you to select a folder on your hard disc in which to store the program.

When downloading of the **Adobe Download Manager** is complete click **Run** to start downloading the actual **Adobe Reader** program. As the program is downloaded from the Adobe Web site you are informed of progress by the window shown below.

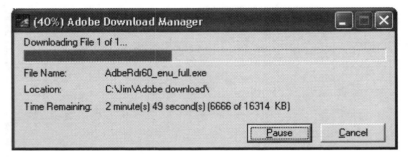

When the download is complete the **Adobe Reader Setup Wizard** is launched automatically.

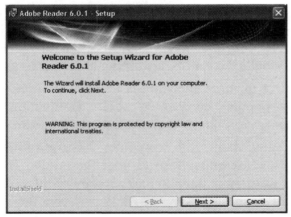

It is now just a case of following the instructions on the screen and mainly clicking **Next** until the program is installed. Finally you are told to restart the computer to complete the process of installing Adobe Reader.

The **Adobe Reader 6.0** program will now be available to run from the *start*, **All Programs** menu on your computer.

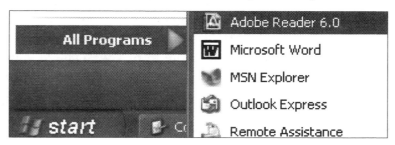

At the time of writing, version 6.0.1 of Adobe Reader is available for free downloading. The Adobe download Web page recommends that you upgrade to version 6.0.2 after installing version 6.0.1. To carry out the upgrade, launch the **Adobe Reader 6.0** program from the *start* menu and **All Programs** as shown above. Then select **Updates...** from the **Help** menu as shown below.

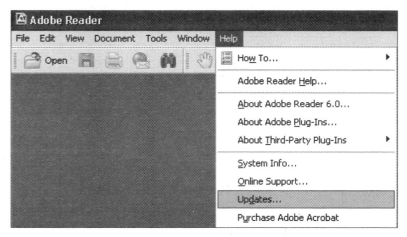

Follow the instructions on the screen to complete the upgrade from version 6.0.1 to 6.0.2.

Using Adobe Reader

There are two ways that you might launch Adobe Reader:

- By selecting **Adobe Reader 6.0** from *start*, **All Programs** (to open an existing PDF document).

- By downloading a PDF file from a Web site to your computer. Adobe Reader normally starts up automatically, displaying the document and allowing you to read through the pages or print the document on paper.

Opening an Existing PDF Document

The first method above would be used if you have an existing PDF file saved on your hard disc or other storage medium. Click **Adobe Reader 6.0** from the *start*/All Programs menu shown on the previous page. The program opens with the menu bar across the top of a blank page. To open an existing document, click the **Open** icon on the left of the menu bar shown below. Then select the required PDF file from the folder on your hard disc or wherever.

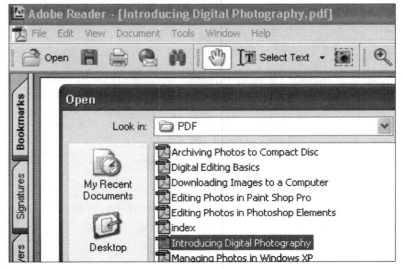

In this example I have selected a PDF file called **Introducing Digital Photography**, a chapter from an earlier book, stored in a folder called **PDF**.

When you click the **Open** button, the page is displayed on the screen rather like a document in a wordprocessor.

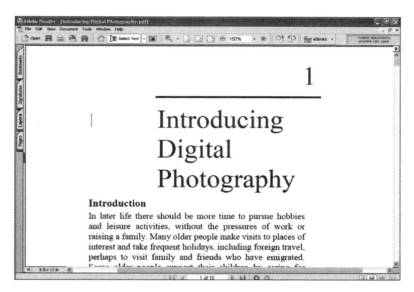

Unlike the wordprocessor, however, the Adobe Reader is essentially a viewing and printing program - you can't edit documents. For editing you need to revert to the original program, such as Microsoft Word, used to create the document in the first place. Then recreate the PDF file using Adobe Acrobat Distiller.

However, as discussed shortly the main purpose of Acrobat Reader is the viewing and printing of documents which other people have created in the PDF format.

Downloading PDF Documents from the Internet

All sorts of organizations make documents available in PDF format for downloading from the Internet. These include Government departments, charities and commercial companies. A good example is the Pension Service which lists a large range of booklets available for downloading in PDF format from its Web site as shown below.

www.pensionguide.gov.uk

Click the link **Print** as shown below on the left in **Print or order our free guides**. A list of a dozen or so guides appears a shown below.

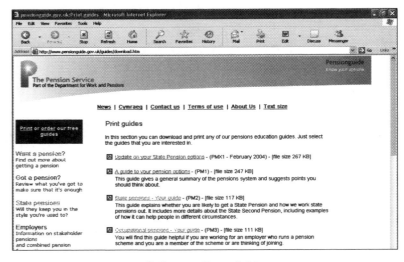

© Crown Copyright

The title of each of the documents listed is a clickable link to allow you to download the guide in PDF format, as shown in the example below.

> A guide to your pension options - (PM1) - [file size 247 KB]
> This guide gives a general summary of the pensions system and suggests points you should think about.

If, for example, you click on **A guide to your pension options** as shown on the previous page, the document is downloaded from the Web site to your computer. Adobe Reader starts up automatically displaying the chosen booklet as shown below.

This particular guide is 40 pages long; you can move through the pages using **Page Up** and **Page Down** on your keyboard. Alternatively use the arrows at the bottom of the screen, as shown below.

Using Adobe Reader

Viewing Options in Adobe Reader

There are several ways of displaying a PDF document on the screen. These are selected by clicking **View** on the Adobe Reader toolbar then **Page Layout**.

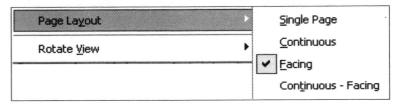

In the example below, the **Facing** page layout has been selected, displaying two pages on the screen side-by-side.

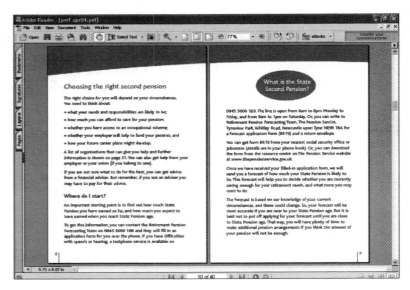

The Adobe Reader Toolbar across the top of the window has many useful options; some of the main ones are shown on the toolbar and discussed below.

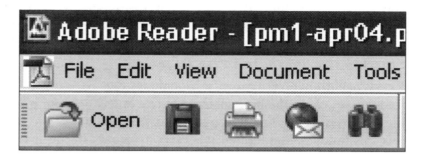

Open an Existing PDF Document

This option allows you to open and display an existing PDF document which is already saved on your hard disc or other medium such as a CD. First find the required folder then select the PDF file before clicking **Open** to display the document on the screen.

Saving a PDF Document (Downloaded from the Web)

The toolbar across the top of the Adobe Reader screen includes an icon to save the document on your hard disc, as shown on the right. Select a folder and give the document a name.

Printing a PDF Document

The **Print** icon shown on the right opens up the Windows **Print** dialogue box ready for you to print the document on paper.

E-mailing a PDF Document

A PDF file can be e-mailed to someone else using the toolbar icon shown on the right. You can either send someone a link to the document on the Web or send the entire document as an e-mail attachment.

Searching for Words in a PDF Document

Every occurrence of a word in document can be found by clicking the binoculars icon and entering the required word. The required word (**SERPS** in this example) is highlighted wherever it occurs in the text and in a list of results.

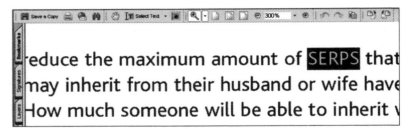

Changing the Text Size in a PDF Document

If you have difficulty reading the text on the screen, Acrobat Reader enables you to zoom in to enlarge the lettering using the toolbar feature shown on the right. In the **SERPS** example above the text has been enlarged to 300%.

Braille Versions of Official Booklets

Please note that the Pension Service Web site also has an online order form for printed copies of booklets, including Braille versions at **www.pensionguide.gov.uk**.

Searching for Information

Introduction

The World Wide Web consists of billions of pages of information stored on millions of computers around the world. Virtually any subject, however obscure, will be covered somewhere – the problem is finding it. Fortunately there are many powerful tools which allow you to search the entire Web rapidly to find the information you require.

Searching Using Internet Explorer

If, like many people, you use the Internet Explorer browser supplied as part of Microsoft Windows, there is a built-in search facility, **MSN Search**, as shown below.

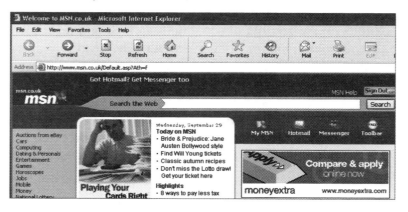

5   Searching for Information

Simply type the subject you wish to search for, such as **winter fuel payment**, for example, into the **Search the Web** bar, as shown below, then click the **Search** button.

A list of results is displayed almost instantly, providing "clickable links" to various helpful Web sites. These give information on eligibility for the payment, advice on applying and payment details. Many of these sites are provided by local authorities.

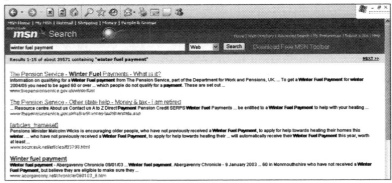

Apart from the **Search the Web** feature built into Internet Explorer, there are lots of separate search programs known either as *search engines* or *directories*. The search engines and directories are commercial enterprises and they charge other firms to advertise on their site. Well-known search facilities include Google, Yahoo!, Ask Jeeves, Lycos, Excite and AltaVista. Many Internet search facilities make use of search engines from other companies. For example, AOL, Excite and Ask Jeeves use Google to power their searches.

The Google Search Engine

The search engine is a special program that allows you to enter *keywords* which are central to the subject you are interested in. **Google** is currently the world's most popular search engine; it's easy to use and quickly finds highly relevant results. It was conceived by two American students, Larry Page and Sergey Brin, at Stanford University in the 1990s. After a modest start in a friend's garage, the business quickly grew so that the two men, still only in their early 30s, are now billionaires, following a recent stock market flotation.

As an example of a search, suppose you were considering releasing some of the capital tied up in your home, perhaps to finance the holiday of a lifetime or to help your children in some way. You might enter the keywords **equity release** into the search engine. Shown below is an extract from the popular Google search engine, with the keywords entered in the search bar.

Note that Google allows you to search for Web pages from the UK or from the entire World Wide Web.

When you click the **Search** button shown above, the search engine scans all of the billions of Web pages and then displays a list of those containing the keywords, in this example **equity release**. An extract from the results of this search is shown at the top of the next page.

5   Searching for Information

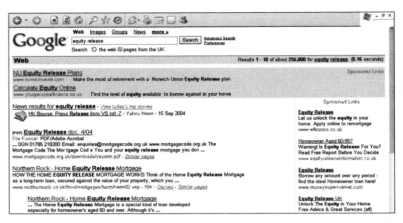

You can see at the top right of the screenshot that Google found about 256,000 results or Web sites containing the words **equity release** and only took 0.16 seconds to find them. The results are displayed in batches of 10 per page.

> Results 1 - 10 of about **256,000** for **equity release**. (0.16 seconds)

The first line of each result is underlined and is in colour. This is a "clickable" *link* leading to a Web page which contains the keywords specified in your search.

> Northern Rock - Home **Equity Release** Mortgage
> ... The Home **Equity Release** Mortgage is a special kind of loan developed especially for homeowner's aged 60 and over. Although it's ...
> www.northernrock.co.uk/html/mortgages/herm/herm01.asp - 20k - 29 Sep 2004 -
> Cached - Similar pages

Of course, you couldn't possibly look at all 256,000 Web sites found by this particular search. Fortunately search engines are cleverly designed to display those Web pages most relevant to your search at the very beginning of the list. So you'll probably find all the information you need on a particular subject by opening the Web pages listed within the first few pages of the results.

Referring to the **equity release** results list on the previous page, clicking on the **laterlife.com** link leads to the **laterlife** site. This covers all aspects of life for older people, including independent financial advice, as shown in the extract below. The principles of equity release are explained and there are also links to professional firms.

www.laterlife.com

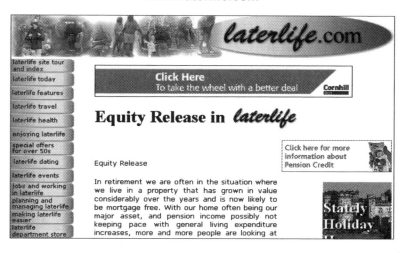

Looking back at the results list on the previous page, you can see, down the right-hand side, a second list of results under the heading **Sponsored Links**, as shown in the extract on the right. The complete list of sponsored links also includes **Which?** reports and firms offering advice on the various equity release schemes.

Sponsored Links

Unlock Your **Equity**
Raise funds by remortgaging your home. Poor credit not a problem.
www.wfinance.co.uk

Homeowner Aged 60-95?
Warning! Is **Equity Release** For You? Read Free Report Before You Decide
www.equityreleaseinformation.co.uk

Equity Release
Use our loan finder to compare over 430 UK loans and apply here!
www.moneysupermarket.com

5 Searching for Information

The **Sponsored Links** connect to companies who pay to have their Web sites listed at the top or side of the list of search results. These are companies providing goods or services which are relevant to a particular search. For the ordinary Internet user, however, the search engine is a free tool; as discussed shortly, you simply type in the Web address (such as **www.google.co.uk**) and start searching.

Apart from basic searching of the entire Web using keywords as discussed previously, Google has many other features. These include searching the latest news, mail order catalogues and groups holding online forums or discussions on a range of subjects.

The **Answers** feature allows you to enter questions to be answered online (for a fee) by a team of researchers.

Using the Directory in Google

The **Directory** section in Google has Web pages organised into categories by human editors, such as **Health** for example, shown below. You can also do a keyword search within a category; this type of search and the resulting list of Web pages will be focused on the relevant subject and not on the entire Web.

Clicking on one of the categories shown above presents a further list of categories. This allows you to find Web pages relevant to your chosen topic. In the example below, **Health** was selected, followed by **Senior Health** and then **Well-Being and Safety**. Shown below is the *thread* or path through the various categories.

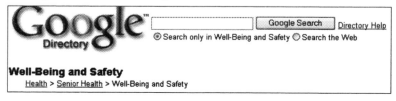

The **Senior Health** category, for example, contains a total of 1134 Web pages, as shown on the right below.

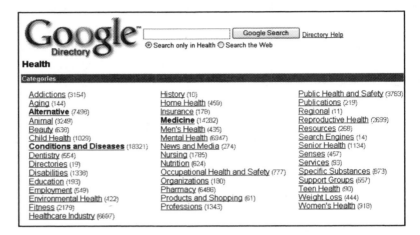

Opening the **Senior Health** category shown below reveals that, for example, there are 26 Web sites on **Well-being and Safety**.

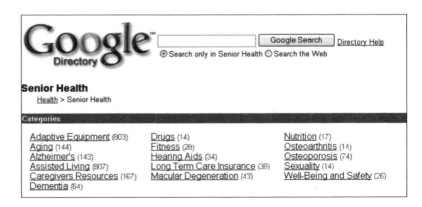

After selecting **Well-Being and Safety (26)** from the **Senior Health** category, Google presents the list of the 26 relevant Web sites in *rank order* as shown in the extract below. (Google decides on the relevance or importance of a site by counting the number of other Web sites which are connected to it via "clickable" links).

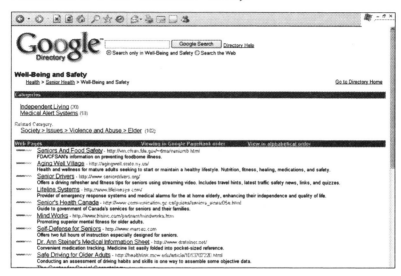

When you click on one of the links (shown underlined above), this opens a Web page, such as the **Mind Works** page, for example, shown below.

Welcome to

MIND WORKS

Promoting superior mental fitness for older adults

Other Search Engines and Directories

Google is currently the most popular search engine, being easy to use and consistently delivering high quality results. However, there are lots of other well-established programs for retrieving information from the Internet, some of which have been around for much longer than Google. Several of these programs are discussed on the next few pages.

Yahoo!

You can start Yahoo! by entering its address into your Web browser (Internet Explorer for example), as shown below. (In practice you don't need to bother typing **http://** at the beginning of an address).

http://uk.yahoo.com/

The **YAHOO! UK & IRELAND** page opens up and you can see that Yahoo! combines features of both a search engine and a directory. At the top is the **Search the Web** bar for entering keywords, as discussed previously in the section on Google. The categories listed lower down the page allow you to find Web pages which have been listed under various headings.

For example, if you select the **Finance** category in **Yahoo!** you are presented with a complete range of up-to-date personal finance information. This includes the latest stock market share prices, as well as comparisons of companies offering savings and investments, loans and car and home insurance, for example. There is also coverage of the latest pensions and housing market news.

Other Yahoo! categories include a **Chat** room, **Sports** features and a facility to search through **Cars** and **Property** for sale. The **Yahoo! GeoCities** feature guides you through the process of setting up and publishing your own Web site.

Ask Jeeves

At first glance Ask Jeeves looks like any other search program, with a clear uncluttered screen and search bar as shown below.

www.ask.com

However, there are several features which distinguish Ask Jeeves from other tools used for searching the Internet. Ask Jeeves is known as a *meta-search engine*, which means it uses several other search engines to obtain the list of Web pages which are relevant to a particular query.

Another feature of Ask Jeeves is that you can enter *questions* in the search bar as well as the *keywords* normally used. For example, you might have heard a lot of publicity about something on the Internet called "eBay" and want to know what it's all about.

When you enter a question, such as **What is eBay?**, the list of Web pages produced is different from the list obtained when you simply enter a keyword such as **eBay**.

On clicking **Search**, Ask Jeeves immediately returns the set of highly relevant results shown below, in response to the search "**What is eBay?**".

You can have a look at some of the Web pages by clicking on the first few links shown underlined above. From these you can quickly find out that eBay is an enormously popular worldwide Internet "auction house". Millions of people buy and sell millions of items every day, from household items such as antiques, china, etc., to cars, motor cycles and even aircraft.

 eBay is the world's largest trading community where millions of people buy and sell millions of items every day.

You might, for example, use eBay to dispose of surplus household items or to get an idea of the value of family heirlooms.

Ask Jeeves has many other features including categories such as news and weather, pictures and products. These can be searched separately.

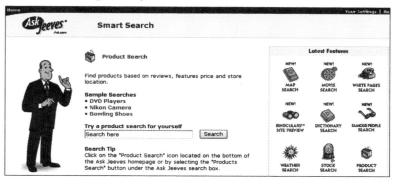

Clicking on the **Products** link on the Ask Jeeves **Home** page opens up the directory with categories leading to Web pages giving details on a wide range of products.

There are many other search engines and directories, some of which have been around since the early 1990s. These include AltaVista (**www.altavista.com**), Excite (**www.excite.com**) and Lycos (**www.lycos.com**).

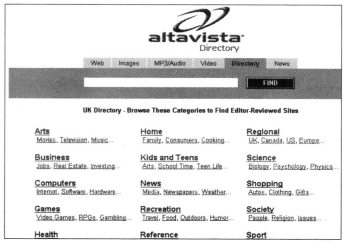

SearchEngineWatch

If you want to find the latest news about search engines, then SearchEngineWatch (**http://searchenginewatch.com**) is well worth a visit.

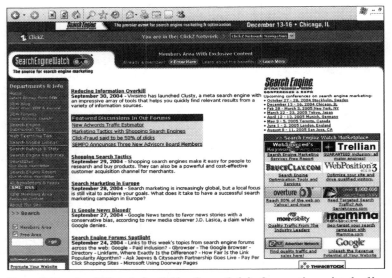

SearchEngineWatch is full of useful information, including tips to improve the effectiveness of your searches, forums to discuss related issues and also the latest news affecting search engines. There are also listings of all the major search engines, detailing their history and essential features. The search engine ratings and statistics feature presents various tables for the popularity of the different search facilities. The **Nielsen NetRatings** provide tables based on the "traffic" using searching facilities and also community networks in different European countries. The **Hitwise Search Engine Ratings** monitor the Internet surfing activities of 25 million people worldwide to produce a table listing the most popular search programs.

Practical Activities

- Have a look at the different search programs by typing their address into your Web browser such as Internet Explorer. The addresses of some of the most popular programs are listed below.

  www.google.com   **www.ask.com**
  uk.yahoo.com   **www.altavista.com**
  www.excite.com   **www.lycos.com**

- Try a few practice searches with each program. Choose some keywords for a subject you are interested in. For example, you might want to find out about your entitlement to the **pension credit**. Which of the search engines produces the most relevant and helpful results?

- Enter a phrase such as **pension credit** into one of the search programs and carry out a search. Then repeat the search with the phrase enclosed in inverted commas, i.e. speech marks as in **"pension credit"**. What effect do the speech marks have on the Web pages found? Try this "phrase search" out on other search programs and see if the effect is the same.

- Use a *directory* such as Yahoo!, AltaVista or the Google directory to find out all you can about a subject such as **cholesterol**, for example. Use a *category thread* rather than a *keyword* search.

- Have a look at **searchenginewatch.com** to find out tips on searching and also the most popular search facilities.

5 Searching for Information

Finding Out About Pensions

The Pensions Shortfall

At the time of writing there is much publicity about a "pensions shortfall", estimated at £57bn, during the first part of the 21st century. Expenditure on pensions has increased because many people are living longer, while at the same time contributions have fallen because early retirement has been commonplace.

Some companies have reduced their contributions to employees' pension schemes or have closed the schemes altogether. Many company pensions have fallen in value in recent years because of the relatively poor performance of shares on the Stock Exchange. Some individuals have lost all or part of their private pension due to financial problems within the company or through pensions mis-selling. The Financial Assistance Scheme has recently been announced by the Government, with £400 million available to compensate anyone in this position. You can find out more about this scheme by carrying out a keyword search in a search engine such as Google.

| financial assistance scheme | Search |

A mixture of strategies is being considered to alleviate the shortfall problems affecting both state and company pensions. These include:

- Encouraging people to save more for their retirement.

- Helping people to continue working (voluntarily) to age 65 or 70.

- Increased taxation.

For the latest reports and information on this subject, obviously of vital importance to many older people, enter the following keywords into your search engine.

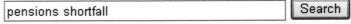

| pensions shortfall | Search |

Amongst the many results of this search is the following extract from the **MYFINANCES** Web site at:

www.myfinances .co.uk

Apart from reports such as the pensions shortfall, the **MYFINANCES** site covers the complete range of financial news and advice including insurance, investment and ways to cut utilities bills such as gas, electricity and telephone.

Searching for Information About Pensions

There are so many different ways of trying to provide for a comfortable retirement – the subject is a minefield of information. For example, there is the *basic state pension*, *occupational pensions*, *personal* and *stakeholder pensions* and *annuities*, not to mention other forms of saving and investment such as property. A simple search in Google (or another search engine if you prefer) produces lots of links to Web sites which give useful advice. Simply enter the following keyword search into your search engine:

In this example, the computer responded with a list of very useful results, as shown in the following extract:

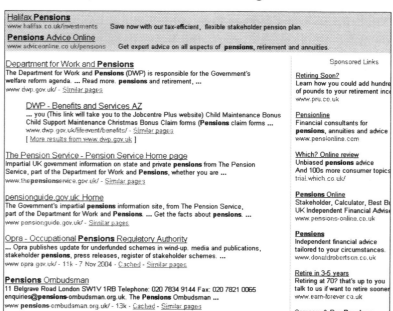

The list of results on the previous page includes links to various government departments and private companies, all giving advice on various aspects of pensions, including both state and private schemes. Down the right-hand side of the previous results list, under the heading **Sponsored Links**, are links to various private companies offering pensions advice and services. These organizations have paid a fee to the search engine company (Google in this example); when you do a search involving pensions, links to the companies' Web sites pop up near the top of the results list.

A good place to start finding out about pensions is the Government's impartial pensions' advice Web site, shown by the link on the previous page, i.e.

www.pensionguide.gov.uk

This site contains further links which allow you to print out or order guide books giving the basic facts about the main pensions issues. There are also descriptions of the various types of pension – state, occupational, stakeholder, etc.

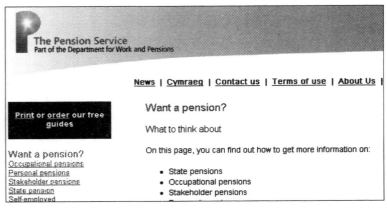

© Crown Copyright

This Is Money

This Web site provides a lot of clear and useful information with news about all aspects of state and private pensions and indeed, personal finances in general.

www.thisismoney.com

As shown above, there are on-screen **Retirement guides** covering the range of state and private pensions. Other topics such as **Equity release** (discussed in Chapter 8 of this book) and **Making a will** are also covered in the guides.

The **BOOST RETIREMENT INCOME** feature gives tips such as looking for **Forgotten Pensions** from previous employment, obtaining work as a supermarket "greeter" and searching for any unclaimed benefits and forgotten savings accounts and insurance policies.

The Pensions Advisory Service

The Pensions Advisory Service has been assisting members of the public since 1983. They provide general information and guidance to members of the public on pension matters. They also help to resolve disputes and complaints about private pensions arrangements (company pensions, personal pensions and stakeholder pensions). Unlike the Pensions Ombudsman, they do not have any statutory powers. They can, however, advise how a complaint can be taken to the Pensions Ombudsman.

The service is free and is sustained by a nationwide network of volunteer advisers who are supported and augmented by a technical and administrative staff based in London. The service is provided via a helpline, written advice, conciliation or by involvement by one of their volunteer professional advisers. All advisers are pension professionals with many years of experience in the pensions industry. They are an independent voluntary organization that is grant-aided by the Department for Work and Pensions.

Their Web site is dedicated to providing general information about company, private and State pensions.

www.pensionsadvisoryservice.org.uk

Stakeholder pensions are covered by their separate Web site at:

www.stakeholderhelpline.org.uk

They can also be contacted by calling their helpline on 0845 601 2923 or writing to The Pensions Advisory Service, 11 Belgrave Road, London, SW1V 1RB.

The Basic State Pension

If you are retired or about to retire, the Pension Service Web site probably contains most of the information you require. The Pension Service is part of the Government's Department for Work and Pensions.

www.thepensionservice.gov.uk

© Crown Copyright

As shown above, the Pension Service Web site contains a **News** section giving the latest information on topics such as the **Winter Fuel** payment and also details of the recently published **Pensions Commission** report. On the lower right-hand side of the Web page shown above is a link to pages giving further information about the **Pension Credit**. This is a scheme by which everyone over 60 is guaranteed a minimum income. The Pension Credit also provides, for the first time, extra income for people who have savings or income of their own, e.g. from a personal pension. The Pension Credit is discussed in detail later in this book.

Getting a State Pension Forecast Online

The amount of basic State Pension you receive depends on how much you have earned over the years. To receive the full basic pension a man needs to pay National Insurance contributions for 44 years and a woman needs to pay for 39 years. The State Pension age is currently 60 for women and 65 for men, but will gradually increase (starting in 2010) until by 2020 it will be 65 for men and women. If you have not yet reached the State Pension age, you can obtain an *online* State Pension *forecast* from the **Pension Service** Web site shown on the previous page. (You cannot obtain a State Pension forecast if you are *within four months* of the State Pension age). The online forecast allows you to obtain answers to questions such as "What if I retire early?" for example.

Click the link **Get a State Pension forecast** on the lower right of the screenshot on the previous

Get a State Pension forecast

e ●●●service

Get a State Pension forecast online

page. For security purposes you must first register for the **Government Gateway**. For this you must enter your name, e-mail address and National Insurance number. Then you are asked to make up your own password and you will be given a **User ID**.

Within a very short time (i.e. the same day) of submitting your registration for the Government Gateway, you will receive an acknowledgement by e-mail. This informs you that your **Activation PIN** will be sent through the post within 7 days, but will expire if not used within 28 days.

www.thepensionservice.gov.uk

www.gateway.gov.uk

Once you have activated the Government Gateway using your newly acquired PIN number, you can fill in your application form for the online State Pension forecast. This requires you to enter (on the screen) details such as your personal status (married or divorced, etc.) and employment status, type of National Insurance contributions paid and birth dates of any children. Then you can submit the forms for obtaining the pensions forecast over the Internet. The calculation of your State Pension forecast takes a very short time – 38 seconds for example.

Then you can print out your State Pension forecast, as shown below, including detailed notes on how the forecast has been calculated and the qualifying years you have accumulated.

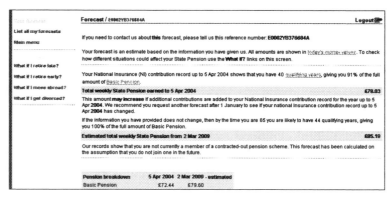

© Crown Copyright

You can ask questions such as **What if I retire early?** or **What if I move abroad?** (as shown on the left of the above screenshot) and find out how your pension is affected.

Having obtained your State Pension forecast, you may decide to make additional voluntary contributions to boost your final pension.

The State Second Pension

In addition to the basic State Pension you may be entitled to a State Second Pension (also known as S2P), previously the State Earnings-Related Pension Scheme (SERPS). SERPS was based on your level of earnings and National Insurance contributions.

In April 2002, SERPS was replaced by the State Second Pension giving a more generous additional State Pension for low and moderate earners. The State Second Pension is also available to some carers and people with long-term disability and illness.

It's possible to "contract out" of the additional State Pension if you have joined an occupational scheme or have a personal pension or stakeholder pension. Contracting out of the additional State Pension scheme will normally mean that you pay reduced National Insurance contributions or receive an annual rebate paid by the Inland Revenue.

It's also possible for a surviving husband or wife to inherit a percentage of their partner's State Second Pension entitlement, up to a maximum of 50%. (The amount of the earlier SERPS pension which a surviving spouse can inherit is on a sliding scale from 50 to 100%).

For more information on the State Second Pension have a look at:

www.direct.gov.uk/

www.thepensionservice.gov.uk

The Pension Service Web site above also includes several booklets on topics such as Contracted-out Pensions and Inheritance of SERPS. These are in the form of Acrobat PDF files which can be viewed on the screen or printed out on paper, as discussed elsewhere in this book.

Finding Out About Other Types of Pension

Apart from the basic State Pension and State Second Pensions discussed previously there are several other pension options available. These include:

- *Occupational pensions* arranged with an employer.

- *Stakeholder pensions* i.e. personal pensions arranged with large banks, etc., according to government rules.

- *Personal pensions* arranged with private companies.

You can find out much more about these types of pension by logging on to:

www.pensionguide.gov.uk

This Web site has links to other pages describing the different types of pension. There are also links which allow you to print or order free guides. You can select from a list the guides you wish to print on paper, as shown below.

Print guides

In this section you can download and print any of our pensions education guides. Just select the guides that you are interested in.

🖹 Update on your State Pension options - (PMX1 - February 2004) - [file size 267 KB]

🖹 A guide to your pension options - (PM1) - [file size 247 KB]
This guide gives a general summary of the pensions system and suggests points you should think about.

🖹 State pensions - Your guide - (PM2) - [file size 117 KB]
This guide explains whether you are likely to get a State Pension and how we work state pensions out. It includes more details about the State Second Pension, including examples of how it can help people in different circumstances.

© Crown Copyright

The guides listed above are saved in a format known as PDF (Portable Document Format) and can be viewed and printed using a freely available program called Adobe Reader, discussed in detail in Chapter 4 of this book.

If you would prefer to obtain the official pension guides in their printed form, you can complete an online order form from the **Pensionguide** page of the Pension Service at:

www.pensionguide.gov.uk

You will need to fill in your personal details and the required number of copies of each of the pension guides.

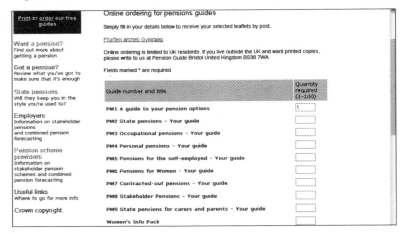

© Crown Copyright

After entering personal details such as your e-mail address you can choose different formats for your copies of the guides, including **Audiocassette** and **Braille**.

Email

Tick here if you do not wish to be contacted in the future   ☐

Which version of the information would you like?*

◉ English
○ Welsh
○ Audiocassette
○ Braille

© Crown Copyright

Comparing Private Pension Schemes

The Financial Services Authority is an independent company which has statutory powers to regulate the financial services industry. Its Web site contains a wealth of useful information, covering pensions and other financial matters. For more information, have a look at:

www.fsa.gov.uk/tables

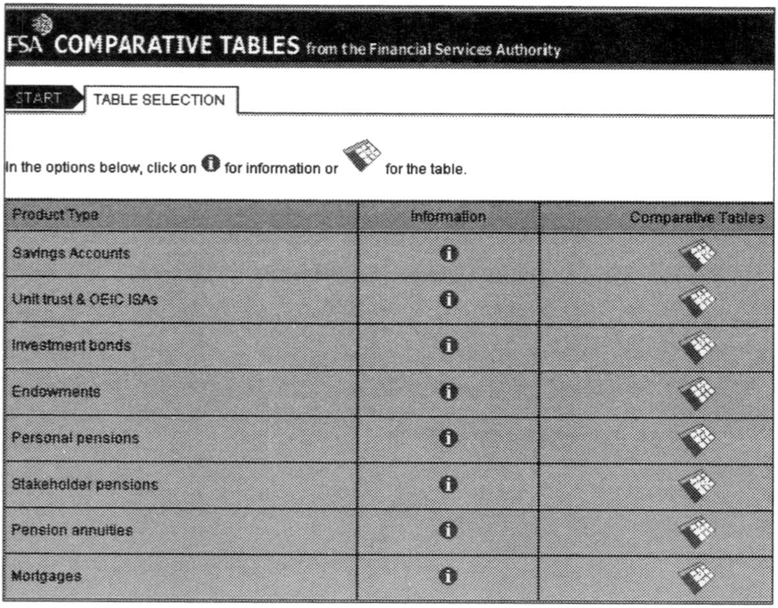

FSA COMPARATIVE TABLES from the Financial Services Authority

START   TABLE SELECTION

In the options below, click on ❶ for information or ▓ for the table.

Product Type	Information	Comparative Tables
Savings Accounts	❶	▓
Unit trust & OEIC ISAs	❶	▓
Investment bonds	❶	▓
Endowments	❶	▓
Personal pensions	❶	▓
Stakeholder pensions	❶	▓
Pension annuities	❶	▓
Mortgages	❶	▓

© The Financial Services Authority

As can be seen above, the FSA Web site covers a wide range of topics from savings and investments to pensions and mortgages. Clicking an icon in the middle column headed **Information** brings up pages explaining each of the **Product Types** listed in the left-hand column.

For example, the following is an extract from the information about **Pension annuities**.

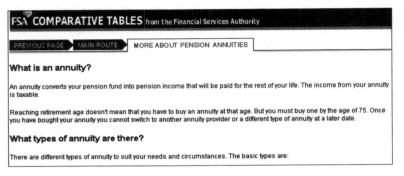

© The Financial Services Authority

The third column on the table on the previous page, headed **Comparative Tables**, allows you to enter your personal requirements for a financial product, such as **Personal pensions**. Then it displays a list of offers from various financial services companies.

© The Financial Services Authority

The extract on the previous page shows a small sample taken from 74 products found in the **FSA Comparative Tables** at **www.fsa.gov.uk/tables** (as at 17/2/05).

The FSA points out that the products described are not recommendations and that all details should be confirmed with the provider or an adviser. The information on any Web site may be subject to change from time to time.

Web Sites Giving Pensions Information

The following is a list of some of the main Web sites giving useful advice and information about pensions.

www.dwp.gov.uk
This is the Government's Department for Work and Pensions Web site, supplying support and advice for people of all ages, including pensioners.

www.thepensionservice.gov.uk
This is the Web site of The Pension Service, a service within the Government's Department for Work and Pensions.

www.fsa.gov.uk
The Financial Services Authority provides many relevant documents, including "Contracting out of the State Second Pension".

www.direct.gov.uk
Directgov is a Web site giving information on a wide range of Government services, including pensions. It is managed by the e-Government Unit, part of the Cabinet Office.

www.pensionsadvisoryservice.org.uk
This is the Pensions Advisory Service. A non-profit making organization staffed by volunteers who have worked as pensions professionals. Provides advice on all aspects of pensions and helps in settling disputes.

www.stakeholderhelpline.org.uk
Pensions Advisory Service site dedicated to helping with stakeholder pensions.

www.fool.co.uk
The Motley Fool Web site gives advice and information on most aspects of personal finance, including pensions.

www.thisismoney.com
This Is Money gives advice and guides on all aspects of state and private pensions and includes an **Advice Bank**, with links to articles on a very comprehensive range of pension topics.

www.adviceonline.co.uk
AdviceOnline is a commercial site, with a statement across the top of the page stating that it is "The UK's Most Popular Independent Financial Advice Site". This site includes several well-presented fact sheets giving information on many aspects of personal pensions such as **Boosting your retirement income** and **Self Employed Pensions**. There is also an online pension projection calculator.

The main charitable organizations also include useful advice and information on pensions, for example:

www.helptheaged.org.uk	Help the Aged
www.adviceguide.org.uk	The Citizen's Advice Bureau
www.ace.org.uk	AGE Concern (Factsheet 19)

Complaints About Pension Schemes

Many complaints concern the way pension schemes are run as shown in this report on the 1Stop Finance Web site.

www.1stop-finance.co.uk

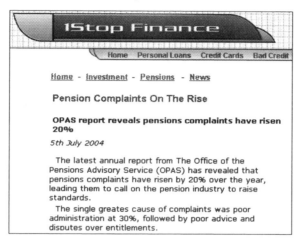

The Pensions Advisory Service has experienced professional volunteers who try to resolve pension disputes by mediation or conciliation.

www.pensionsadvisoryservice.org.uk

The Pensions Advisory Service may advise you to take your case to the Pensions Ombudsman, an independent adjudicator with statutory powers to investigate and settle disputes about pension schemes.

www.pensions-ombudsman.org.uk

Complaints about the selling and marketing of private pension schemes are dealt with by the Financial Ombudsman Service.

www.fos.org.uk

The Pension Credit

As mentioned earlier in this book, the amount of basic State Pension anyone receives depends on their National Insurance contributions throughout their working life. The Pension Credit is a scheme which guarantees a minimum income to everyone aged 60 and over. The Pension Credit is administered by The Pension Service, part of the Government's Department for Work and Pensions.

The Pension Credit takes the form of a weekly payment in addition to any existing pensions and benefits. From April 2005, everyone over 60 was guaranteed a minimum income, (known as the Guarantee Credit) of at least:

> £109.45 a week if you are single
>
> or
>
> £167.05 if you have a partner

There is also extra money (called the Savings Credit) for people over 65 who have saved or provided themselves with an extra income for their retirement.

You can still benefit from the Pension Credit even if you are already receiving some other benefits. For example, the Attendance Allowance (discussed shortly) is a benefit paid to anyone who needs extra care. The Attendance Allowance is ignored in calculating entitlement to the Pension Credit. You can find out more about the Pension Credit by clicking the link (shown below) on the Pension Service Web site at:

www.thepensionservice.gov.uk

The Pension Service Web site gives full details of the Pension Credit including eligibility and the types of allowances and benefits which are not counted as income.

www.thepensionservice.gov.uk

Types of income that are not counted include:

- Attendance Allowance
- Disability Living Allowance;
- Housing Benefit; and
- Council Tax Benefit

© Crown Copyright

There are also sample calculations, such as the following, which shows how savings above £6000 are taken into account. Each £500 of savings is assumed to be equivalent to an income of £1 per week. (Savings below £6000 are ignored in calculating the Pension Credit).

Example 2 - Balbir and Manju

Balbir and Manju are both 75. Their weekly income is as follows:

State Pension (Balbir)	£79.60
Retirement Pension (Manju)	£79.60
Personal pension (Balbir)	£12
Savings of £8,000 (we assume £1 of income for every £500 or part of £500 for any savings over £6.000.)	£ 4
Total weekly income	£175.20

Pension Credit will give them £14.52 a week extra. As a result their total weekly income will increase to £189.72

© Crown Copyright

Please note that the Pension Credit figures quoted in this chapter are correct at the time of writing but are set to rise by 13 per cent by April 2008.

The Pensions Service Web site contains **Guidance Charts**, selected from the **Pensions Credit** page.

www.thepensionservice.gov.uk

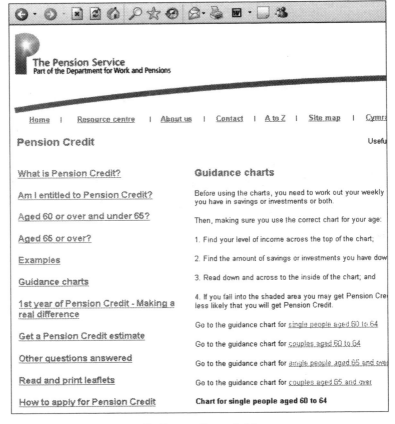

As shown in the following example, the guidance charts are displayed on your screen, allowing you to estimate, at a glance, whether you are likely to qualify for the Pensions Credit.

First you choose, from several charts, the chart appropriate to your age and personal status, i.e. single or one of a couple. Then you find the point on the graph which corresponds to your **Weekly income** read off the horizontal scale and **Savings and investments** read off the vertical scale. This will show whether you are **Less likely** or **More likely** to receive the Pension Credit.

Chart for couples aged 60 to 64

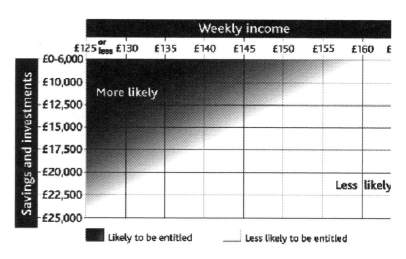

© Crown Copyright

6   Finding Out About Pensions

The Pension Service Web site also provides an online
calculator to estimate the amount of any Pension Credit to
which you may be entitled. You are required to enter
details of your personal circumstances, including details of
any savings, income and benefits.

	You	Your partner
	£ per week	£ per week
State Pension	49	0
Occupational / private pension(s) - this includes payments you receive from your former employer on account of early retirement due to illness or disability. (these could be from your or your partner's previous employer)	£ per week 30	£ per week 15

© Crown Copyright

After entering all of your personal details your Pension
Credit *estimate* is calculated and displayed as shown in the
following fictitious example.

Pension Credit Calculator

Results page

Based on the information you have given us today, you may be entitled
to a Pension Credit payment of **£118.20** per week.

This is based on the following information:

- You are 65 or over.
- Your partner is under 60.
- You have savings of £2,500.00.
- No one else lives with you.
- You have an outstanding mortgage of £50,000.00.

© Crown Copyright

There are three ways to apply for the Pension Credit. You can phone the **Pension Credit application line** using the number given on the Web site as shown below. Or you can print out an application form from the Web site and fill it in by hand. The third alternative is to fill in the application form online, then print it and post it to the Pension Service.

Pension Credit Application form

You can apply for Pension Credit **by freephone** by calling the **Pension Credit application line** 0800 99 1234, textphone 0800 169 0133 (8am to 8pm Monday to Friday, 9am to 1pm Saturday).

Or, you can complete an application form and post it to your pension centre free of charge.

Pension Credit application form – to print out and fill out by hand - [PDF file 432kb]
you can also use an interactive version of this form, which you can complete on screen, then print out and post.

Pension Credit application form to fill out on screen, and then print - [PDF file 1.01mb]

The address of your local Pension Service office can be found from the Pension Service Web site by selecting **Contact** then entering your post code under **Contact Us**.

If your query is about **Winter Fuel Payments** or the **One-off 70+ Payment**, contact the Winter Fuel Payment Helpline.

Contact us

Find out which of our offices you should contact by entering your postcode below.

What is your enquiry regarding? | Pension Credit ▾ |

Enter your postcode | DE656N | Go   Clear

After clicking **Go** the computer responds by displaying the address of your nearest Pension Service office. There are options to print out the official leaflets online.

Pension Credit guides

Pension Credit – Pick it up it's yours (English) [PC1L] - [PDF file size 3.38mb]

Pension Credit – Pick it up it's yours (Welsh) [PC1LWales] - [PDF file size 952kb]

If you or your partner are 60 or over, you could be entitled to Pension Credit – a new entitlement which will be introduced in October 2003. This guide explains what Pension Credit is and how you can claim.

A Guide to Pension Credit [PC10S] [PDF file size 317kb]

This guide is for people who want to know more about Pension Credit, such as professional and voluntary advisers.

These are in Adobe Acrobat PDF format as discussed in Chapter 4 in this book.

There are several other Web sites giving useful information about the Pension Credit, including Age Concern who publish from their Web site a number of factsheets and information sheets. Factsheet 48 is a 28-page document in Adobe Acrobat format which can be downloaded and printed from the Age Concern Web site at:

www.ace. org.uk

(Please see the notes on downloading and printing Adobe Acrobat files elsewhere in this book).

The Citizens Advice Bureau also publishes information on the Pension Credit at:

www.adviceguide.org.uk

This site also includes information on other benefits, as discussed shortly, and is updated on a monthly basis.

Benefits for Older People

The Unclaimed Millions

Many older people may be able to improve their standard of living by claiming all of the benefits to which they are entitled. Every year hundreds of millions of pounds go unclaimed for various reasons. The Internet is the ideal medium to find out what benefits are available and who is eligible. The following keyword search provides some interesting information on this subject.

pensioners unclaimed benefits	Search

The following extract from the **This is Money** financial Web site, states that pride is preventing many pensioners from claiming their entitlements, such as the pension credit.

www.thisismoney.co.uk

thisismoney.co.uk
Money made easy

Armageddon for the grocers
from the publishers of Daily

◀ Back to home
▶ News
▶ Investing & markets
▶ Insurance
▶ Money savers
Money savers guides
Message boards
▶ Retirement
▶ Saving & banking
▶ Mortgages & homes

money savers

Pride robs elderly of extra money
Jane Wallace, Daily Mail
29 May 2004

PENSIONERS are still missing out on state benefits, although the Government claims its new pension credit system is a success.

According to the Department for Work and Pensions, 2.4 million households receive the new.

OTHER STORIES

A Case Study

Mrs. A had reached the age of 87 years with little or no help from the state, other than the basic old age pension. She and her late husband had run a small farm for nearly 50 years until retiring. Mrs. A took great pride in being independent – she had always been very careful with money and saved for her retirement. The idea of claiming benefits was alien to her, even though she had always conscientiously paid Income Tax and National Insurance. In any case, filling in lots of claim forms and trying to understand all of the jargon and red tape was just too much at her time of life.

However, disability caused by two major operations and a progressive illness meant that Mrs. A needed to rely increasingly on her daughter, who had no qualms about claiming genuine entitlements from the state. Furthermore, Mrs. A's daughter was computer literate, so it was possible to find out from the Internet exactly what benefits were available. In some cases it was also possible to print out the application forms and information leaflets "online".

Using information from the Internet, Mrs. A's daughter was able to secure several substantial state benefits for her mother, namely:

> Pension Credit (an addition to the basic pension).
>
> Attendance Allowance.
>
> Reduced Council Tax.

These amounted to a very significant increase in weekly income and therefore quality of life for Mrs. A. In addition, Mrs. A's daughter was also able to obtain a carer's allowance for looking after her mother for at least 35 hours per week.

Some benefits, such as the Pension Credit (covered in the last chapter) are available even if you have quite substantial savings.

As discussed on the following pages, there is a wealth of helpful information on the Internet on all of these subjects. Various government departments and private companies now place their information leaflets on the Web as a matter of course. Charitable organizations such as Age Concern also publish useful information on the Web. Many of these Internet documents are very clearly written in plain English and help to cut through much of the "red tape" which often makes official documents so confusing.

For example, if you want to print out leaflets explaining the **Pension Credit**, this can be done from **The Pension Service** Web site, after clicking on one of the links shown below.

www.thepensionservice.gov.uk

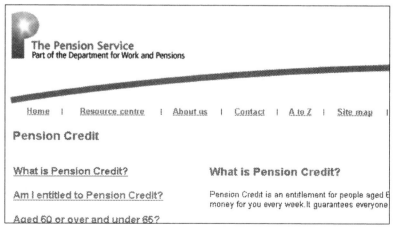

© Crown Copyright

Benefits Available to Older People

It's perhaps not surprising that many benefits go unclaimed – there is a bewildering number of benefits available. Many people, I would imagine, will need some help in order to find out all of the benefits to which they are entitled. This is where the Internet is invaluable, for not only can you find lists of all of the benefits available but also read detailed notes on eligibility and methods of applying. This is far easier than traipsing round Government or council offices or post offices to find all the benefits leaflets. A search in Google (or similar search engine) is all that is required.

(If you enter "**benefits for pensioners**" in Google, the "**for**" is ignored, as are similar common words). The list of results from this search includes links to Web sites provided by government departments, charities and many local authorities, as shown below.

DWP - **Benefits** and Services AZ
... Guide (This link will take you to The **Pensioners** Guide website ... to the Jobcentre website) Poland – Your social security insurance, **benefits** and healthcare ...
www.dwp.gov.uk/lifeevent/**benefits**/index.asp - Similar pages
[More results from www.dwp.gov.uk]

Age Concern England - Age Concern urges **pensioners** to claim (04.04
... The campaign encourages **pensioners** to claim the **benefits** they are entitled to as new increases in social security **benefits** come into force on Monday (April ...
www.ageconcern.org.uk/AgeConcern/news_903.htm - 26k - Cached - Similar pages

Benefits for **pensioners**
... BENEFITS FOR PEOPLE AGED OVER 60 ATTENDANCE ALLOWANCE (AA). • p
have. AA may entitle you to extra money on other **benefits**. DISABILITY ...
www.nottinghamcity.gov.uk/coun/ department/social_services/welfare/**pensioners**.asp
17 Nov 2004 - Cached - Similar pages

Among the links on the previous page is one to the Web site of Nottingham City Council, for example.

www.nottinghamcity.gov.uk

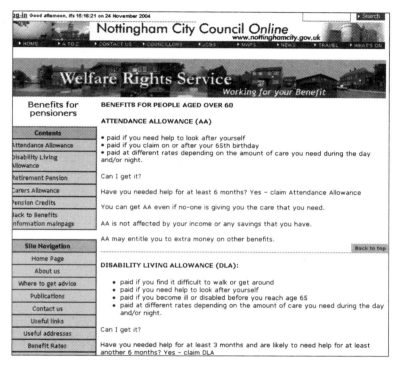

Down the left-hand side of the Web page shown above is a list of some of the main benefits available to pensioners. These include **Attendance Allowance, Disability Living Allowance, Carers Allowance** as well as the **Retirement Pension** and **Pension Credit**. In the centre of the page is a description of each of the benefits and notes to help you decide if you are eligible.

7   Benefits for Older People

The Web site of Greenwich Council gives a listing of most of the benefits available to older people.

www.greenwich.gov.uk

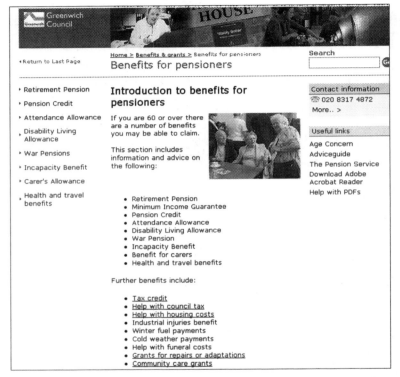

Each of the benefits listed on the left-hand side above is a link to a more detailed description of the benefit, with notes on eligibility and methods of claiming. On the right of the above Web page are links to Age Concern and Government departments such as the Pension Service. There is also a link to enable you to down load a copy of the Adobe Reader program, enabling you to read and print copies of official booklets, as discussed elsewhere in this book.

The **Association of Retired and Persons Over 50 (ARP050)** is the UK's leading social and campaigning membership organization for people over 50. Benefits of membership include discounts (10% on average) on goods and services from leading stores and companies. There are news features and a help section which includes notes on some of the main state benefits which may be available to people over 50 if they are eligible.

www.arp050.org.uk

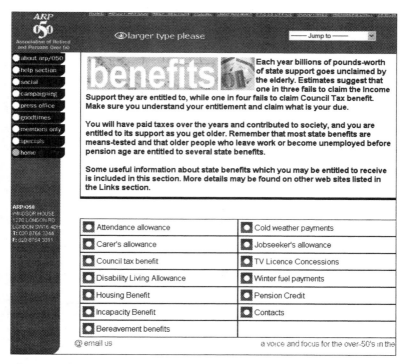

If you click on any of the benefits listed above, an outline of the benefit is displayed, giving the amounts of any payments, eligibility and who to contact to make a claim.

7 Benefits for Older People

For a complete listing of benefits and services, have a look at the Government's Department for Work and Pensions Web site, as shown in the extract below.

www.dwp.gov.uk

© Crown Copyright

Click the link **benefits and services A-Z** as shown above to display the full list of benefits and services, extending over several pages. A small extract is shown below.

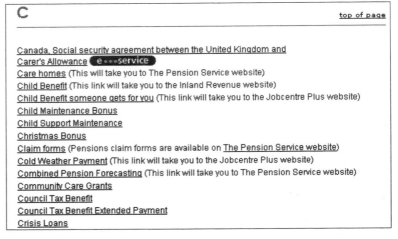

© Crown Copyright

There is also guidance and downloadable booklets for people living abroad; for example how to receive benefits and your British State Pension while living in another country.

The following list of benefits, mainly for older people, has been extracted from the **benefits and services A-Z** as shown on the extract on the previous page, located at the Web page **www.dwp.gov.uk**.

Attendance Allowance

Bereavement Allowance

Bereavement Payment

Carer's Allowance

Christmas Bonus

Cold Weather Payment

Council Tax Benefit

Disability Living Allowance (DLA)

Funeral Payment

Housing Benefit

Incapacity Benefit

Income Support

Medical treatment and care for War Pensioners

New Deal for people aged 50 plus

Over 50

Over 80 Pension

Pension Credit

Pensioners' Guide

Retirement

Severe Disablement Allowance (SDA)

War Disablement Pension (Veterans Agency)

War Widow's Pension (Veterans Agency)

Winter Fuel Payments

To find out more about any of the benefits listed on the previous page, log on to the Department for Work and Pensions Web site at **www.dwp.gov.uk** and select the **benefits and services A-Z** section as discussed previously. Each of the benefits listed is a link to a Web page giving detailed information. This describes the purpose and amount of each benefit, the rules for eligibility, how to make a claim and how payments are made.

If you want to look at a variety of alternative Web sites giving information on any of the benefits listed on the previous page, carry out a search by entering the name of the benefit into a search engine such as Google.

In the above example, clicking **Search** produces a list of results including links to various Web sites giving information on Council Tax Benefit. These are provided by government departments, charitable organizations such as AGE Concern and various borough and district councils.

The next few pages look in more detail at some of the main benefits which may be claimed by many older people and which can produce a substantial increase in living standards. These are:

- Attendance Allowance
- Disability Living Allowance
- Carer's Allowance.

(Another important benefit, the Pension Credit was discussed in the previous chapter).

Attendance Allowance

This is a benefit paid to anyone over 65 who needs help with personal care due to mental or physical illness. (People under 65 can claim the Disability Living Allowance, discussed below.) This benefit is not means-tested so you will get it even if you have substantial savings. Although this benefit is paid to anyone needing the attendance of a carer or helper, you can still receive the benefit even if no-one actually attends.

Currently there is a *lower rate* of Attendance Allowance for anyone needing care either in the day *or* at night (£39.35 per week); anyone needing help both day *and* night receives the *higher rate* of Attendance Allowance of £58.80 per week. Recipients of Attendance Allowance must have needed help for 6 months prior to receiving the benefit; the terminally ill receive the benefit as soon as their condition is diagnosed by a doctor.

Disability Living Allowance

This allowance is paid to people between ages 16 and 65 who have special care and mobility needs. It is intended to help with the additional costs arising from severe disability and illness. DLA continues after age 65 but no new claims can be made after this age.

The Disability Living Allowance is paid regardless of any savings you may have and, like the Attendance Allowance above, does not depend on National Insurance Contributions having been paid. The DLA is paid, even if the person involved is not actually receiving any care. DLA is paid at 3 weekly rates for *care needs* i.e. £15.55, £39.35 and £58.80. *Mobility needs* are paid at a lower rate of £15.55 and a higher rate of £41.05 weekly.

To find out more about the Attendance Allowance and Disability Living Allowance, have a look at:

www.dwp.gov.uk
The Web site of the Department for Work and Pensions.

www.benefitsnow.co.uk
This Web site has online questions allowing you to assess yourself for benefits such as Attendance Allowance, Disability Living Allowance, etc.

www.benefitsandwork.co.uk
This Web site provides free guides on the main benefits and allowances and there are also online discussion groups. This site also lists short courses for people with various conditions and also for their carers and support workers.

www.rnid.org.uk
This is the Web site for RNID, including a benefits information factsheet for deaf and hard of hearing people. There are factsheets on the full range of benefits including Attendance Allowance and Disability Living Allowance. These can be downloaded and viewed or printed in Adobe Acrobat (PDF) format as discussed elsewhere in this book. Alternatively ready-printed versions can be ordered online.

www.direct.gov.uk
This site has a great deal of information about the complete range of Government services and some very helpful explanations of the Attendance Allowance, Disability Living Allowance and Carer's Allowance (discussed shortly). Claim packs enabling you to apply for these benefits are downloadable in Adobe Acrobat (PDF) format as discussed elsewhere in this book. There are also telephone numbers for ordering ready-printed copies including Braille and large print versions.

www.bhas.org.uk

This is the Web site of the Barton Hill Advice Service, a registered charity providing help for people in the East Bristol area.

The site provides a wide range of advice and downloadable guides for people with physical disabilities, mental health problems and problems affecting older people. There is a link to allow you to download a copy of Adobe Reader (essential for reading and printing many downloadable Internet documents in PDF format, as discussed elsewhere in this book.)   The Barton Hill site also includes some online **five minute tests** to allow you to see if you (or perhaps someone in your care) may be eligible for the Attendance Allowance or the Disability Living Allowance.

Are you looking for help on?:
Disability Living Allowance for children.

Try our five minute tests
To see if your child might be eligible for DLA:
Physical or **Mental** health test.

For Adult:
Try the test for DLA claims: **Physical** or **Mental** health test.

If you are over 65 you may qualify for **Attendance Allowance: try the AA test**

What people say about our guides:
"Excellent guide to claiming DLA. As an adviser for a disability advice bureau I found this guide extremely useful and the availability of this online will allow us to provide copies free of charge to our clients. Well done."
Calderdale D.A.R.T. (Disabled Advice Resource Team), Halifax.

Read more feedback >>
Send feedback >>

Carer's Allowance

If you are looking after a disabled person for at least 35 hours a week, you may be eligible for this allowance. The disabled person needs to be receiving Attendance Allowance or Disability Living Allowance. It is not affected by any savings you may have. Currently the Carer's Allowance is £44.35 per week. Since October 2002, a carer over the age of 65 can qualify for the Carer's Allowance. Anyone over 65 who wishes to claim may be entitled to the Carer's Allowance from that date, but not before.

It's possible to claim the Carer's Allowance online using the Government's **e-service** mentioned earlier in this book.

Log on to the Department for Work and Pensions Web site at **www.dwp.gov.uk** and select the **benefits and services A-Z** section as discussed previously. Now select **Carer's Allowance** from the **A-Z** list as shown in the extract below.

C   top of page

Canada, Social security agreement between the United Kingdom and
Carer's Allowance (e···service)
Care homes (This will take you to The Pension Service website)
Child Benefit (This link will take you to the Inland Revenue website)
Child Benefit someone gets for you (This link will take you to the Jobcentre Plus website)
Child Maintenance Bonus
Child Support Maintenance
Christmas Bonus

© Crown Copyright

Then on the next screen select **Claim Carer's Allowance online**. You will then be able to start a new online claims form, where you will need to enter your National Insurance number, details of the person you are caring for and your bank, building society and any employment details.

Discounts and Special Offers for Older People

The previous pages covered some of the main state benefits available to older people. You can also save money by looking for special offers and discounts for older people. You might try entering a search such as the following example using Google.

For example, the Association of Retired and Persons Over 50 mentioned earlier obtains discounts for it members on a wide range of goods and services, as shown by the following entry in the results of the above search.

www.arp050.org.uk

Association of Retired and Persons **over 50** -
... By encouraging everyone **over 50** to make the most of life, we aim to ... substantia
broadened the range of member benefits, services and **discounts** and opened ...
www.arp050.org.uk/asp/about/history.asp - 4k - Cached - Similar pages

Association of Retired and Persons **over 50** -
... a **50%** discount off weekend stays at **over** 110 Comfort, Quality, Sleep and
and Inns. Britannia Hotels The UK is even more available as **discounts** ...
www.arp050.org.uk/asp/about/benefits.asp - 13k - Cached - Similar pages

Also included in the results list for the above search is a link to the Laterlife Web site, shown on the next page.

www.laterlife.com

Special Offers for the **Over** 50s
... Special rates for the **over 50's** during July and August 2002 ... National Express
offers 30% **discounts** on most National Express services for **over** 50s ...
www.laterlife.com/laterlife-special-offers2.htm - 37k - Cached - Similar pages

UK Life Insurance, Travel Insurance, Home Insurance
... in the **50-65** age range. Home Insurance. Cornhill Insurance are offering on
for Home Insurance with some remarkable **discounts** for **over** 50s. ...
www.laterlife.com/laterlife-insurance-section.htm - 26k - Cached - Similar pag

7 Benefits for Older People

The Laterlife Web site includes special offers for the over 50s, including travel, insurance and hotel accommodation.

Discounts on Rail Travel

The **Senior Railcard** (costing £20 per year) allows people over 60 to get a third off rail fares in the UK, while the **Rail Senior Card** (costing £12 annually) gives 20% off rail fares across Europe. The **Disabled Persons Railcard** (£14 per year) allows a travelling companion to receive a discounted fare too.

www.senior-railcard.co.uk
www.disabledpersons-railcard.co.uk
www.railcard.co.uk

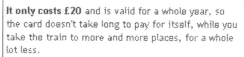

Travel begins at 60

Welcome to the Senior Railcard site. If you are aged 60 or over, you are automatically eligible for a Senior Railcard enabling you to travel all over England, Scotland and Wales at **1/3 off most First Class and Standard fares**.

It only costs £20 and is valid for a whole year, so the card doesn't take long to pay for itself, while you take the train to more and more places, for a whole lot less.

Discounts on Coach Travel

The National Express coach company offers the **routesixty** scheme allowing anyone over 60 to travel at half-price on most of their coach routes. There's no need to pay for a special discount card.

www.nationalexpress.com

routesixty

Take to the road
for half the price!

Over 60? Then you automatically qualify for our routesixty fares. They mean you can travel for half-price on most National Express services.

Even on days when half-price fares aren't available, a routesixty fare will still get you a great discount.

There's no need to pay for a discount card like there is on the railways – everybody over 60 is entitled to half-price travel.

Saving on Gas and Electricity Bills

There are many Web sites providing online information and price comparisons of different suppliers of utilities such as Gas and Electricity, with claims of savings of £170-£200 per year on your bills. To see a few examples, enter the following into your search engine and click **Search**.

The list of results includes independent organizations offering advice, as well as companies offering to find you the cheapest suppliers of gas and electricity according to your postcode. The process of switching supplier can be completed online in just a few minutes.

There is a code of practice for the above companies administered by the independent "watchdog" **energywatch**, who also give lots of advice on energy on their Web site.

www.energywatch.org.uk

For impartial advice about saving on energy and heating in the home, look at the Citizen's Advice Bureau's Web site. Select **Housing** and **Energy efficiency and saving money**.

www.adviceguide.org.uk

The Powergen Staywarm scheme allows people over 60 (in qualifying households) to pay a fixed price, no matter how much gas and electricity is needed during the year.

www.staywarm.co.uk

The Age Concern Web site provides factsheets on topics such as **Help with heating**.

www.ace.org.uk

8

Managing Your Money

Introduction

The Internet is an ideal medium for obtaining financial advice and information. For example, anyone with savings usually wants to look around and find the best rates of interest. In order to get the whole picture you might traditionally have looked at a variety of newspaper advertisements and articles; I even heard of one elderly lady who actually travels around various midland towns by bus, physically visiting banks and building societies to seek out the best offers.

The Internet makes it possible to obtain financial advice and information in your own home at any time of the day or night. Interest rates are liable to change from time to time but a Web site is able to display the latest information almost immediately. This is because a bank or building society only needs to update the information in a single place – their Web site stored on a central *server* computer in their computing centre. This single up-to-date source of information can then be viewed by all of the customers whenever they go online – much simpler then distributing thousands of leaflets and newspaper advertisements.

You can now put any spare money into *online savings accounts*; these generally pay a better rate of interest since they are cheaper to administer than a traditional branch-based account. The online customer in their own home is doing much of the work previously done by the banks' staff working in the branch. In addition, much of the paperwork has been eliminated. As discussed later, some Internet bank accounts can also be used for various banking functions such as transferring money, paying bills, printing statements, setting up standing orders, arranging loans and overdraft limits and ordering foreign currency. Contrary to what some people might believe, Internet accounts are actually a very safe home for your money, provided a number of simple and effective security precautions are followed, as discussed later in this chapter. In the last resort, the large banks and building societies usually guarantee that customers won't lose money in the event of fraud, unless the customer has been negligent.

The Age Concern Web site contains a lot of information about taxes and savings for older people. The Web site has a book section, including **Your Taxes and Savings 2004-2005**, by Paul Lewis who has broadcast regularly on financial matters on BBC Radio 4. The book states that pensioners are losing many millions of pounds each year through paying too much tax and explains ways of avoiding this. Another section explains how to get the best return on savings and there is advice on the Financial Services Authority and ways of dealing with complaints and claims for compensation. The book can be ordered online from the Age Concern Web site.

www.ageconcern.org.uk

Finding Out About Interest Rates on Savings

Enter a keyword search such as **savings interest rates** into a search engine such as Google, as shown below.

The Internet responds with the following results.

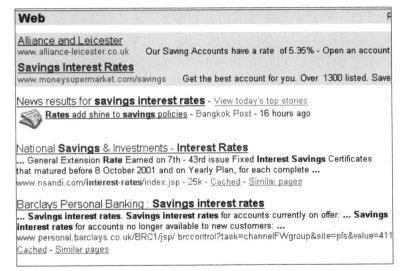

Many of the results are links to the Web sites of the large banks or building societies, such as the Alliance and Leicester and Barclays. There is also a link to National Savings and Investments, which offers savings bonds and certificates backed by HM Treasury.

Financial Advice Web Sites

Some of the previous results are links to financial advice Web sites which include tables comparing interest rates for all of the major organisations. Some of these are shown under the heading **Sponsored Links,** as shown on the right. These are companies that have paid to have links to their site included in the results of searches involving savings.

Sponsored Links

Top **Savings** Accounts UK
Highest **interest rates** detailed.
Find the best **rates** at a glance.
www.about-savings-accounts.co.uk

Compare UK **savings**
accounts. Compare over 1000
products. Earn over 6% **interest**.
www.moneyexpert.com

Compare **Savings** Accounts
Find Great **Rates** & Saving Offers
From Leading UK Companies.
www.e-shopping.co.uk

MoneyExpert

The **MoneyExpert** site compares over 1000 financial products.

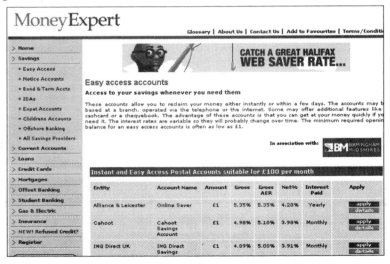

(Interest rates quoted in this book applied at the time of writing but will subsequently change from time to time).

Please note that the **MoneyExpert** Web site shown on the previous page actually extends to 16 pages of tables. For each account there is a button to click for more information and a second button which opens up an online application form. If you are not very familiar with the jargon of the financial world, the **MoneyExpert** Web site also has a useful A-Z glossary of financial terms, accessed by the button shown on the right.

www.moneyexpert.com

MoneyExtra

This is a financial Web site offering advice and information across the complete range of financial services, including **Savings & Investing** and **Pensions & Retirement**. As shown below, there are features giving comparisons of different types of account, such as **Deposit Accounts, Cash ISAs** and **Stocks and Shares ISAs** from over one hundred providers.

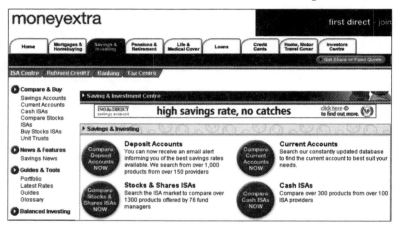

The **MoneyExtra** site includes a glossary of financial terms and online guides to investment. As shown below, the Investment Centre provides a complete range of share management tools including the very latest stockmarket prices. There is an online share dealing service and you can get instant e-mail alerts when your shares rise or fall.

www.moneyextra.com

This is Money

This financial Web site includes a comprehensive range of advice and information, with a **Money Shop** comparing financial services such as over 300 bank accounts and 1,400 savings accounts. The **Retirement** section reports on the latest news affecting pensioners and **ASK A QUESTION** allows you to enter, online, a financial question (savings, pensions, tax, etc.) to be answered by a team of experts.

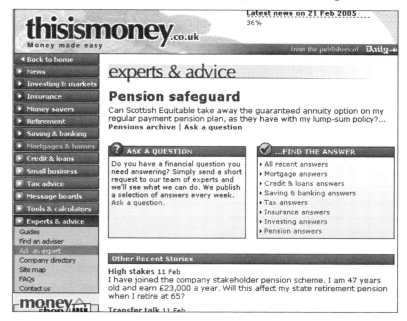

This is Money includes a message board where members can discuss problems and share advice about financial issues. For example, one member asked how a mainstream bank could allow his grandfather to leave £60,000 in a *current* account, earning no interest.

www.thisismoney.co.uk

The Motley Fool

This site includes the complete range of financial information already discussed, such as comparisons of savings accounts and online share dealing.

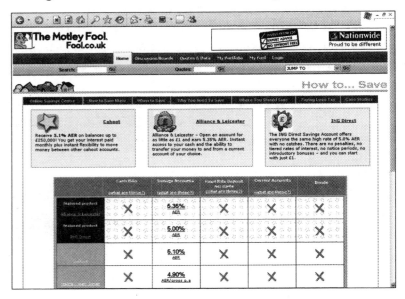

At the time of writing, free membership of The Motley Fool entitled you to the Fool's Top Ten Money Tips and there were also free guides on topics such as ISAs and getting out of debt.

www.fool.co.uk

Internet Bank Accounts

It's now possible to carry out many of your banking activities from the comfort of your own home. There's no longer any need to travel to a branch unless a face-to-face meeting is really necessary or you need to withdraw actual cash in the form of notes.

Obviously many people will be concerned about security, but reputable organisations guarantee that in the event of fraud, customers won't lose any money. Internet security is discussed in more detail later, but one of the main security methods is to *encrypt* (or encode) all information sent between your computer and the bank's computer. Even if the information were fraudulently intercepted it would not be intelligible to the criminals.

To participate in *online banking*, you obviously need a computer and modem and an account with an Internet Service Provider. To find out more about online banking, log on to the Web sites of any of the major banks, such as the Halifax, at **www.halifax.co.uk** and the Bank of Scotland, at **www.bankofscotland.co.uk**.

Once online to the bank you will find lots of information about the range of services offered. A major advantage of online banking is that you can access your accounts at almost *any time of the day or night* – there's no need to wait for normal banking hours.

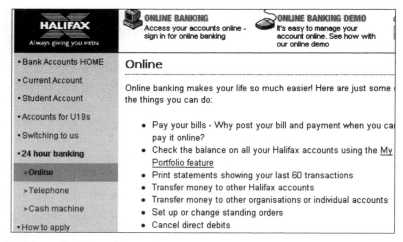

With online banking you will be able to carry out most of the normal banking functions, such as:

- View your balance
- Print a statement
- Pay bills
- Transfer funds between your various accounts
- Transfer money to another person's account
- Set up standing orders
- Apply for an increased overdraft
- Check and cancel direct debits
- Order foreign currency.

The Web sites for the Halifax and Bank of Scotland both have links leading to demonstrations which give you a tour of the online banking service. The extract below from the Bank of Scotland, shows how recent transactions can be viewed on the screen or printed as a statement.

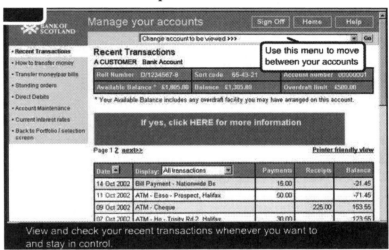

Once you have signed up for online banking, your bank will arrange with you a *user name* (sometimes also called a *login name* or a *user ID*) and a *password*. Shown below is the login screen for the Halifax Online Service.

You may be asked to provide at least one additional piece of security information, such as a parent's name, some memorable piece of personal information or a secret question and answer. If you forget your password there is usually a number to ring to arrange a new one. At this time the additional security information is used to prove your identity. Obviously all security information such as passwords, etc., should be kept safe and not written down and left in obvious places.

Once you have opened an online bank account you can view your list of accounts. This gives an overview of your various accounts with the bank, displaying your total financial position on one screen. At the Halifax, this is known as **My Portfolio**, shown below.

The portfolio lists not only your bank accounts, but also details of any share dealings, investments, mortgages, credit cards and saving accounts, etc.

The **Halifax Financial Portfolio** and the various online services are accessed via the menu shown below.

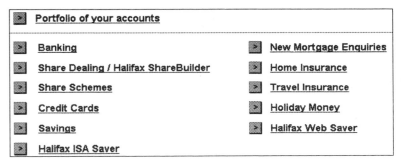

You can also open new accounts, such as the Halifax Web Saver shown below. Internet savings accounts may offer interest rates above those generally available with conventional savings accounts.

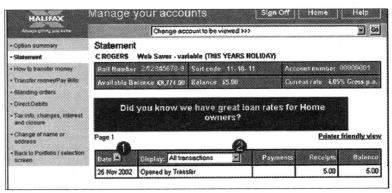

As shown above, although the Web Saver is an investment account paying interest, it also enables bills to be paid and money to be transferred to an account with a different bank.

Security of Online Bank Accounts

Carrying out financial transactions over the Internet is bound to be a cause for concern. Online banking involves sending and receiving personal financial information between your computer and that of the bank. Internet shopping and paying for goods online requires us to give our credit card details to suppliers. Fortunately, reputable businesses like the big banks and established suppliers have strict security systems to prevent fraud. In the unlikely event of a fraud occurring, the best organizations guarantee that customers won't lose money. There are also many simple precautions which individuals can take to make fraud difficult.

Passwords

As well as a *User Name*, you will be issued with (or choose your own) *Password*. This should not be something obvious like the name of a pet or family member. Although your password doesn't appear on the screen (usually replaced by a line of dots, etc.), beware of anyone looking over your shoulder while you type it.

- Never leave your password lying around, in fact don't write it down at all.
- Don't walk away and leave the computer open at your bank account. Some systems log you out if the computer is not used for 10 minutes
- Always *log out* or *sign off* when you have finished using the computer.
- Don't give anyone your user name or password.
- Change your password regularly.

Security Software

Make sure your computer has a *firewall* installed. This is a piece of software which stops hackers from gaining access to your computer and possibly interfering with your bank accounts.

A *virus* is a program maliciously designed to invade your computer and cause damage. Some banks, etc., provide their online customers with virus protection software. Otherwise *anti-virus software* packages such as Norton AntiVirus, McAfee VirusScan and Dr. Solomon's Anti-Virus Toolkit are relatively inexpensive. Make sure your computer has a firewall and anti-virus software – large companies protect their own *server* computers in the same way.

Secure Servers

Servers are the computers used by banks and other large organizations to hold the details of millions of transactions and customers' accounts. *Secure servers* use *encryption* to prevent criminals from accessing financial or confidential information sent between computers. Encryption scrambles or encodes the information so that it can only be decoded or made intelligible by authorized users.

Organisations such as banks and large suppliers use an encryption level known as *128 bit SSL (Secure Sockets Layer)*. Whenever you are online to a secure server, a small closed padlock icon appears at the bottom right of your screen. Double-click the padlock icon to reveal details of the security certificate issued to the company. Always deal with companies who use secure servers.

Raising Money from Your Home

Even in later life, when children may have left home and the property may be paid for, there is sometimes a need to raise a substantial amount of cash. You may wish to finance the holiday of a lifetime, improve your home, buy a new car or possibly help your children or grandchildren in some way. The prospect of repaying a normal bank loan out of a modest retirement income may not be desirable or even feasible. Credit cards are very expensive and other forms of borrowing may be extremely risky and costly.

Anyone owning their own home has seen the value of the property escalate rapidly in recent years. Even a modest house can now be worth hundreds of thousands of pounds in certain areas. Many older people are therefore sitting on a substantial fortune, even though their income and spare cash may be quite modest. The expression "asset rich – cash poor" probably applies to more people than ever, particularly with the general decline in the value of shares and pensions in recent years.

Not surprisingly many older people now consider unlocking some of the built-in value or *equity* in their homes. After all, why live in abject poverty if there is a large untapped pot of cash at your disposal. In any case, at the time of writing, nearly half of the value of any assets over £275,000 (including your home) will go in Inheritance Tax when you die, as discussed in the next chapter. (£275,000 was the Nil Rate Band for Inheritance Tax introduced in April 2005, increasing to £285,000 in April 2006 and £300,000 in April 2007).

The next few pages look at Web sites giving advice and information about ways of raising money from the value of your home.

Moving to a Smaller Home

When the children have left home, an older person may not need a large house with surplus bedrooms. Why not move to a smaller place and raise a substantial amount of cash in the process? If it's your own or main home that you're selling, the surplus cash will be tax-free for you to spend in any way you like. A smaller home will be cheaper to heat and easier to maintain and the Council Tax will be less. A family home with a large garden may become a considerable burden as you get older and less active and gardening help can be particularly expensive. Moving to a smaller home should give you the time and money to do the things you want to do. The process is sometimes called **downsizing**; the same term is also used when people of all ages leave the "rat race" to live a simpler life and also when large companies shed employees.

To find out more about downsizing in later life, enter the following into a search engine such as Google.

In the above search, it is necessary to use the keywords **older people home downsizing** to make the results more relevant. If you simply enter **downsizing** on its own the results will contain lots of links to companies going through a downsizing process.

Shown below are the results of the downsizing search from the previous page.

Web	Results 1 - 10

the issues of ageing
... Many **older people** who might previously have been offered a **home** in specialised accommodation such as a residential care **home** or nursing **home** as a consequence ...
www.3rdagehomes.bartlett.ucl.ac.uk/ homepg/issofage-fold/poverty-fold/adapt.html - 21k - Cached - 5

the issues of ageing
... Staying put' schemes offer **older people** help with ... improvement of their homes in order to help them to continue to live an independent life in their own **home**. ...
www.3rdagehomes.bartlett.ucl.ac.uk/ homepg/issofage-fold/poverty-fold/staying%20put.html -
[More results from www.3rdagehomes.bartlett.ucl.ac.uk]

[PDF] National Service Framework for **Older People** 1 Notes of the sixth ...
File Format: PDF/Adobe Acrobat - View as HTML
... Nancy Davies expressed concern that **older people** were often prevented from **downsizing**, as the cost of new homes marketed as retirement properties were often ...
www.wales.nhs.uk/sites/ documents/439/ipg_mins_110604-e.pdf - Similar pages

Find a Property - Property Is Pension For Many
... **Downsizing** Bungalow builders will be pleased to hear that ... they will move to a smaller **home** when they ... a growing population of active and affluent **older people**. ...
www.findaproperty.com/cgi-bin/story.pl?storyid=5881 - 13k - Cached - Similar pages

Some of these links are to companies involved in the property business while others are Government organizations such as the NHS. At least two of the sites warn that if downsizing continues to grow as expected in future years, the value of smaller homes suitable for both retirement and first time buyers will increase in relation to larger family homes, thus reducing the possible gains from downsizing.

The **Find a Property** Web site shown on the next page has articles describing the housing and living options for older people, stating that many people are using their property as a way to boost their dwindling pension pot.

www.findaproperty.com

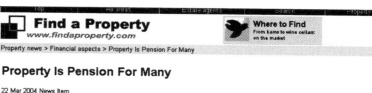

Find a Property
www.findaproperty.com

Where to Find
From barns to wine cellars: on the market

Property news > Financial aspects > Property Is Pension For Many

Property Is Pension For Many

22 Mar 2004 News Item

Unhappy with their dwindling retirement pot, many Britons are turning to property to boost their pension...

According to research carried out by Birmingham Midshires, property is being viewed by ma as the pot of gold at the end of the retirement rainbow - either to fund a place in the sun, place in the country or to provide money through equity release.

Tim Hague, Head of Savings and Investments at Birmingham Midshires, says: "People are searching for ways to give their retirement savings a boost. But our research has shown a increasing number of people see their home as a 'get out of jail free' card.

"Equity release schemes and downsizing to smaller homes are sensible options for some people, but no one should rely upon their home. Houses are not immune from price fluctuations and people should not have all their eggs in one basket.

"We would advise people to regularly review their retirement savings. Start to save as earl as possible - and we appreciate this is not always easy."

RETIREMENT OPTIONS

The **Find a Property** (**www.findaproperty.com**) Web site shown above also describes schemes such as **Equity Release** (discussed shortly) and moving abroad, where property may be much cheaper.

An article entitled **Silver Service** on the **Find a Property** Web site describes the growth of the market for specialist retirement properties. These may be houses or apartments, for lease or for sale. There are retirement villages with all the usual amenities such as doctors, libraries, shops, etc., allowing independent living but with discreet security and emergency services to support an older population.

Factors against downsizing are discussed on the Aviva Web site. This quotes a Norwich Union Report (promoting equity release as an alternative to downsizing). The report emphasizes the emotional attachment of people to their family home and garden and mentions the stress of leaving behind family memories and friends and neighbours.

www.aviva.com

Selling Part of Your Garden for Building

If you have a large garden, one possible way to raise money is to sell a building plot. This might raise anything from about £40,000 up to several hundred thousand pounds, depending on the location and the size of the plot. The following search finds some useful information.

The rather long list of keywords **selling part of your garden for building** is necessary to eliminate a lot of irrelevant results. (In practice, Google ignores common words like **of** and **for**). Several of the sites listed in the results discuss the pros and cons of selling a building plot. For example, if the land is part of your principal residence you should not usually have to pay Capital Gains Tax on the proceeds, although there are exceptions, depending on the size of the plot and the way it has been used in the past. Also, if you sell the main house first, the building plot will then be subject to capital gains tax. Disadvantages include the loss of privacy, a possible decrease in the value of the main property and potential conflict with angry neighbours.

The advantages of selling a building plot include the fact that you stay in your own home with a substantial pot of cash and a smaller garden to look after. Not everyone these days wants a large garden, so selling off a building plot may not damage the value of your house too seriously. These and other points are discussed in detail on the Guardian Unlimited Web site.

www.money.guardian.co.uk/property

Retiring Abroad - A Place in the Sun

Many of us dream of moving to a warm climate to escape the British winter. The price of properties in some European countries is a fraction of similar places in the UK, so you could raise a substantial amount of cash by moving abroad. You might even be able to keep your British home and buy a second home abroad and earn some income from holiday lettings. To find out more about this subject enter the following into your search engine.

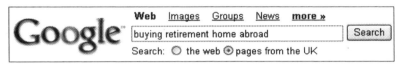

The results of this search include lots of companies offering properties abroad for sale. However, there are many possible pitfalls in buying a property abroad and these are explained in some of the Web sites listed in the results of the above search. For example, the **Tax Consultants Guide** Web site points out that properties abroad may not rise in value as much as those in the UK and may also be difficult to sell. Property and land taxes may be substantial in some countries compared with Britain; foreign laws and legal documents may be difficult to understand and very different from the British legal system. A bi-lingual lawyer or translator may be necessary for your transactions.

www.taxconsultantsguide.com

The Guardian Unlimited Web site discusses moving abroad and compares the relative costs of buying property in different European countries, including expenses such as stamp duty, mortgage rates, legal fees and capital gains tax.

www.money.guardian.co.uk/movingoverseas

Equity Release

If you really want to stay in your home but need to raise a large amount of cash, then one of the many equity release schemes may be for you. At the time of writing, the poor performance of pensions combined with recent increases in property prices makes this a very tempting way of funding major projects or enhancing your retirement. One estimate puts the value of over 65s homes at over £1,100bn and the equity release "market" is predicted to reach £5bn by 2010.

To participate in equity release you generally need to be over 55 or 60 and own your home outright or have a very small mortgage. There are two common types of scheme, (which can raise up to 75% of the value of the property):

1. You receive an interest-only loan based on the value of your house. When you die the house is sold and the loan paid off.

2. You sell a share of the home to a company who pay you a lump sum or a regular income. When you die the house is sold and the lender gets their share.

As shown on the next page, there are many Web sites offering advice on equity release schemes and many companies promoting them. You need to get good independent advice before embarking on such a scheme; this would include discussing your plans with trusted professional advisers, friends and relatives, including any intended beneficiaries of your estate. Firms in the business of selling equity release schemes may highlight the advantages and gloss over or ignore any drawbacks. In the same way, companies selling retirement homes may emphasise the advantages of downsizing to a small bungalow and fail to mention any negative consequences.

Several of the Web sites discussed below give impartial advice on both the risks and the advantages of equity release schemes. Enter the term **equity release** into your search engine, as shown below.

This search finds a huge number of very relevant results, reflecting the amount of activity in this burgeoning business.

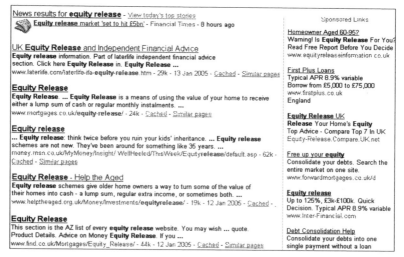

As shown in previous searches on different topics, the results of the above search provide links to various types of organization. These include charities like Help the Aged and also financial Web sites giving independent advice. Finally there are the commercial companies selling equity release schemes, as listed under **Sponsored Links** above.

Help the Aged

The well-known charity includes a section on equity release, with a list of pertinent questions (and answers), such as **How much money will I receive?** and **Will I be able to live in my home for the rest of my life?** There are notes on the regulation of equity release schemes and the **SHIP Code of Practice**, discussed below.

www.helptheaged.org.uk

Age Concern

This charity produces free factsheets and information sheets on the complete range of issues affecting older people. Factsheet 12 is **Raising Income and Capital from Your Home** and covers **Equity Release**, amongst other things. These are in the Adobe PDF format, as discussed in Chapter 4 of this book, downloadable from the Age Concern Web site.

www.ace.org.uk

laterlife.com

This site includes an article describing equity release and outlining the risks, including the danger of rising interest rates adding to the debt and wiping out the equity.

www.laterlife.com

SHIP- Safe Home Income Plans

This is a company, set up by leading providers of home income and equity release plans, to protect planholders. Plans conforming to the **SHIP Code of Practice** display the **SHIP** logo on any printed material. This guarantees, amongst other things, that you cannot lose your home – whatever happens to the stock market or interest rates.

www.ship-ltd.org

Earning Money

You don't have to be a couch potato when you reach the age of 50. Of course, if you're able to retire on a healthy pension you can probably afford to spend a lot of time travelling to exotic places, playing golf or pursuing a hobby such as oil painting, photography or gardening. However, because of the pressure on pensions, there is every indication, at the time of writing, that many people will be forced to keep working for longer, perhaps even until the age of 70. Obviously no-one of that age could be expected to cope with life rushing about the motorways, or doing a demanding manual job or working in a stressful business or professional environment.

However, as this chapter attempts to show, there are opportunities for people over 50 to obtain congenial employment, perhaps on a part-time basis. This might also provide companionship, mental stimulation and the extra cash needed to afford a decent standard of living. Here are a few examples from my own experience:

- I was able to retire from teaching in my early fifties and have supplemented my pension for 10 years by writing books such as this one.

- A neighbouring couple have run a very successful dog kennels business for 20 years since retiring.

- A local dealer in caravans pays retired people to travel to Europe and drive back new motor caravans – thus combining travelling with earning an income.

- A friend in his 70s supplements his pension by building and repairing computers, having taught himself the necessary skills since retiring.

There are lots of articles about employment for older people, as the following search shows.

This search led to the following list of links to Web sites.

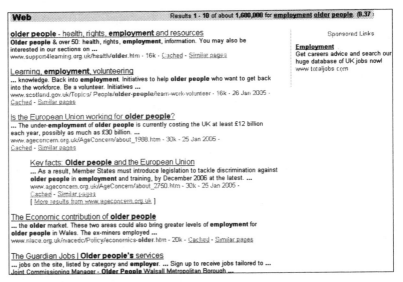

Many of the Web sites listed above highlight the problems of age discrimination by employers. A report on the **Age Concern Web** site states that there are 3.5 million unemployed people in the 50-65 year old population and of these 890,000 say they would like to work.

www.ageconcern.co.uk

However, the fact that few are companies listed under **Sponsored Links** on the previous page suggests a lack of interest in older people by companies.

A report on the Web site of the **National Audit Office** lists the barriers to employment such as age discrimination by some employers, low confidence and low levels of skills. The report also states that the Government's **New Deal 50 Plus** has helped more than 120,000 people obtain employment.

www.nao.org.uk

Help the Aged has a feature **Age Discrimination at Work** which highlights the fact that 90 percent of older workers feel that employers discriminate against them. Also mentioned is a lack of legal protection for older workers and preferential treatment given to younger employees. The **Help the Aged** Web site mentions that in October 2006 legislation will be introduced as part of the European Employment Directive to ban age discrimination in the workplace. Companies making an effort to employ older people are mentioned.

www.helptheaged.org.uk

The Web site of the Scottish Executive discusses their **Training for Work** programme which can help people over 50 and also the national **learndirect** service for the acquisition of vocational skills. There are also links to the **Code of Practice on Age Diversity in Employment** and the **Age Positive** Web sites which oppose age discrimination in the workplace.

www.scotland.gov.uk

www.agepositive.gov.uk

www.learndirect.co.uk

Self-Employment for Older People

As shown on the previous pages, there are still battles to be fought to end age discrimination by employers. Also, many of us who spent half our lives working for large organizations are undoubtedly happier working for ourselves in later life. There's no-one to fall out with and you can choose your own hours of work. On the negative side, it is often solitary and your income may be variable. However, self-employment is the chosen option of many of the over 50s. In fact, it has been reported that over one third of the UK's entrepreneurs are over 50.

The Age Concern Web site discusses **PRIME**, "the UK's only organization built to boost 50+ 'olderpreneurs'". While acknowledging that starting a new business can be a risky business, PRIME offers loans of up to £5000 and help to enable older people become self-employed, such as advice about benefits, training courses and business advice. Examples are given including pet training, music recording and Web and graphic design.

PRIME is a subsidiary company owned by Age Concern with the backing of HRH The Prince of Wales.

www.primeiniative.org.uk

www.ageconcern.org.uk

The Government scheme **New Deal 50 Plus** can provide advice and support and even a regular income for older people taking training courses with a view to becoming self-employed.

www.over50.gov.uk

9
Legal Matters

Introduction

Most people would probably agree that when it comes to the major legal issues in life it is prudent to consult a reputable solicitor. Matters such as buying and selling a house or getting a divorce may be too risky to be resolved without professional advice. Similarly, other legal issues which become more important in later life may also justify the services of experienced professionals. However, as this chapter attempts to show, there is a huge amount of advice available on the Internet which can be very useful in providing you with a sound basic knowledge of important subjects. This may be helpful if you do eventually consult a lawyer or other professional, for the following reasons:

- You won't need to ask basic questions or listen to explanations at an elementary level.

- Having a working knowledge of a subject will help you to state clearly your requirements, may avoid problems and possibly save time and money.

- Any professionals you deal with will be impressed if you have prepared yourself well and this should enable any meetings to be more productive. You will be less likely to be hoodwinked if you have the misfortune to consult a corrupt practitioner.

9 Legal Matters

Some of the main legal issues of particular importance to older people are:

- Drawing Up a will
- Inheritance Tax and Trusts
- Registering a death
- Arranging a Funeral
- Probate, Executors, etc.

At first glance it might seem that the Internet would have no relevance to such traditional matters. However, as shown in the next few pages, there is a wealth of up-to-date information on the Internet about all of these subjects. Much of this material has been provided by professionals – experts in their particular field. Furthermore, you can read the advice from a large number of experts, not just the one nearest to your home.

The Internet is a single source of information on a wide range of subjects – you don't need to consult several different organizations to find out the basic facts. There is no need to get on a bus or jump in the car and travel to the relevant office – it all comes to you in the comfort of your own home. For some tasks, such as applying for probate, as discussed later, you may be able to download application forms from the Internet and print them on your computer. This should be much easier and quicker than waiting for them to be sent in the traditional letter post.

Finally, some of the legal tasks which inevitably occur in later life must be carried out at times of great distress. At such times it may be very helpful to be able stay at home and find advice from the Internet instead of having to travel around or make lots of phone calls.

Finding Out About Wills

A very productive search can be carried out by simply entering the keyword **wills** into your search engine.

On clicking the **search** button the following results were displayed.

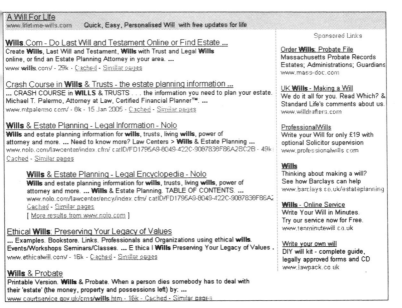

As usual the results include a variety of companies and organizations offering advice and services. These include an online will writing service, **wills.com**, and numerous other businesses. There is an offer of help from one of the big High Street banks and a DIY will kit from Lawpack Publishing Limited.

The **Last Will and Testament Kit** can be ordered in printed form and there is also a CD-Rom version to allow wills to be printed on your computer. The Web site quotes the names of solicitors firms who have approved the kit. Articles on many aspects of making wills are included and warnings about the dangers of intestacy (dying without leaving a will) are given. There is a list of frequently asked questions about wills and probate and a glossary of legal terms. The Web site states that complicated legal issues should always be referred to a qualified solicitor and there is a link to a database of lawyers provided by the Law Societies in Britain.

🔘 Find a lawyer

Complicated legal issues should always be referred to a qualified solicitor. Search for local legal advice here.

www.lawpack.co.uk

Age Concern

The Age Concern Web site includes the downloadable **Factsheet 7 – Making your will**. The document is in the Adobe Acrobat PDF format as discussed in Chapter 4 of this book. Factsheet 7 is an 8-page document and covers many aspects of wills, including Inheritance Tax and what happens if you don't make a will. You are advised to consult a solicitor if your affairs are complicated and also to contact the local Citizens' Advice Bureau if you need further help. The Age Concern Web site also points out that the cost of drawing up a will depends on the complexity of the estate and that a solicitor may make a home visit if it is more convenient.

www.ace.org.uk

Directgov

This Web site has pages covering all Government services, including **Making a will**. There are links to other helpful sites such as **Age Concern** and the **Citizens Advice**.

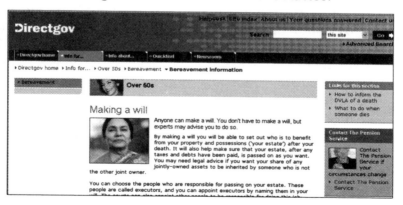

© Crown Copyright

www.direct.gov.uk

laterlife.com

This Web site has a section on legal matters under the heading **planning and managing laterlife**. The **Clickdocs** feature allows you to order ready-made wills, of which there are four standard types, depending on your circumstances, i.e. with or without children or married and unmarried. These standard wills can be customized to suit individual requirements. The **laterlife.com** Web site also includes a guide to various aspects of wills such as **Why write a will**, **Executors**, **will disputes**, **Alterations to a will**, **Inheritance tax**, **Mirror Wills** and **Storage of your will**. There is a charge for each document, which can be downloaded to your computer for editing in Microsoft Word and Works. Editing includes inserting the names of the people to be mentioned in the will.

www.laterlife.com

The Association of Retired and People Over 50

As mentioned elsewhere, this is a campaigning organization for people over 50. The Web site contains a legal section with sub-sections including **Making a will**, as well as other related topics such as **Dealing with death**, **Bereavement benefits** and **Prepaid Funerals**. Making a will gives some warning about the dangers of not making a will and also the problems arising from DIY wills. There are tips about preparing to see a solicitor and some discussion about topics such as Inheritance Tax, Enduring Power of Attorney and Living Wills. Links are provided to other Web sites such as Age Concern, the Society of Will Writers, and the RNIB, who can provide large print, Braille and tape guides to making a will.

www.arp050.org.uk

Inheritance Tax

Many of the older generation will pay 40% Inheritance Tax on part of their estate when they die. Inheritance Tax is currently levied on all estates over a certain value – £275,000 at the time of writing in 2005; please also see the note at the bottom of this page. Recent property price increases mean there are lots of people with ordinary houses who now have estates valued at well over that figure. Then there are the chattels, i.e. possessions such as furniture, car, etc., to be added to the estate. So the dependents of many ordinary people, not usually considered rich, could well be faced with an Inheritance Tax bill of £50,000 – £200,000 or more.

£275,000 (or whatever is the current figure) is known as the Nil Rate Band; although this has increased recently, property prices have soared in comparison, bringing more and more people into the Inheritance Tax net when they die. In the past the seriously rich were forced to find ways of reducing Inheritance Tax, previously known as Capital Transfer Tax and Estate Duty. However, people of more modest means can avoid paying some of the Inheritance Tax by careful planning. For instance, a husband and wife *each* have a tax free allowance equal to the Nil Rate Band of £275,000. When the first partner dies, they could (if they can afford it) give their children a tax free sum up to the Nil Rate Band. This reduces the size of the estate by up to £275,000 so that when the second partner dies, there is less Inheritance Tax to pay. This would effectively save over £100,000 in tax.

(£275,000 is the Nil Rate Band for Inheritance Tax from April 2005, increasing to £285,000 in April 2006 and £300,000 in April 2007).

Enter the keywords **inheritance tax** into your search engine such as Google.

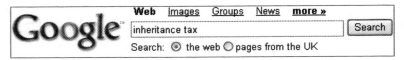

Not surprisingly this is a hugely productive search reflecting the size of the Inheritance Tax "planning" (i.e. avoidance) industry.

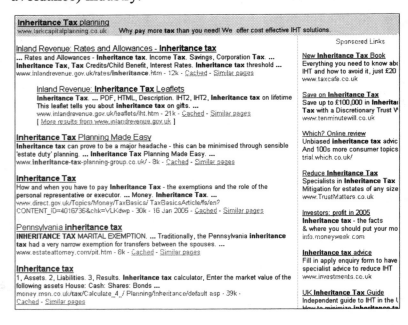

Many of the results are links to companies offering to show you how to avoid paying Inheritance Tax. Some results are links to Government departments such as the Inland Revenue and Directgov. Then there are the financial and consumer Web sites offering advice and information.

The Inland Revenue

This Web site gives the Inheritance Tax threshold, i.e. Nil Rate Band, which is £275,000 at the time of writing increasing to £300,000 in April 2007. The Inland Revenue Web site lists about 16 leaflets on Inheritance Tax; these can be viewed on the screen as Web pages or downloaded in Adobe PDF format as discussed in Chapter 4 of this book. The leaflets include help to calculate Inheritance Tax and notes on estates which may be excepted.

www.inlandrevenue.gov.uk

Tax Café

One of the **Sponsored Links** in the Inheritance Tax search is to the **Tax Café** Web site, shown right. This includes a book, **How to Avoid Inheritance Tax**, written by a chartered accountant specializing in taxation. The book can be purchased online then downloaded in Adobe PDF format and read on the screen or printed on paper. Alternatively you can order a printed copy. The book is written in a very readable style covering many aspects of IHT. For example, the book describes **Lifetime Exemptions** in which a person can give away up to £3000 a year. (Husbands and wives can each give this amount). This amount is tax free no matter how long you live. However, if you give away a larger sum and die within 7 years, some IHT will be due, depending when you die. Various types of Trust which reduce Inheritance Tax are also described.

> Sponsored Links
>
> New **Inheritance Tax** Book
> Everything you need to know about IHT and how to avoid it, just £20
> www.taxcafe.co.uk

www.taxcafe.co.uk

Discretionary Trust Wills

One of the results of the previous search on Inheritance Tax was to a site named the **10MINUTEwill**. This site gives a very detailed description of a popular and legal way of minimizing your Inheritance Tax bill. This allows married couples to make full use of their £275,000 allowance and is known as the **Nil Rate Band Discretionary Trust**.

The Nil Rate Band was £275,000 from April 2005 increasing to £300,000 by April 2007.

As mentioned earlier, a husband or wife could simply give away assets up to the £275,000 allowance when the first one dies, thus reducing the estate when the second partner dies. Transfers of assets between husband and wife are tax free. However, after the death of the first partner, the remaining partner will be poorer by up to £275,000; this may be a problem if the survivor lives on for many years.

The **Nil Rate Band Discretionary Trust** allows the first partner to leave up to the Nil Rate Band in trust, for the eventual benefit of the children or grandchildren, say. However, the surviving spouse continues to have some control and benefit from the £275,000 left by the deceased partner, while possibly avoiding £100,000 in tax.

The **10MINUTEwill** includes a lot of help on this subject, including a downloadable Adobe PDF document. You can write a **Nil Rate Band Discretionary Trust will** online, by inserting standard paragraphs and it is stated that every possible permutation of will that can be generated by the software has been checked by a qualified solicitor.

www.tenminutewill.co.uk

You should always consult a qualified solicitor if your affairs are complicated or you have any doubts.

When Someone Dies

Dealing with a death is probably the worst situation which most of us ever have to face. In the short term there are legal formalities to be carried out such as obtaining a death certificate, registering the death and arranging the funeral. In the case of an estate involving property above a certain value it is necessary for the executors appointed in the will to obtain a Grant of Probate. This allows the assets of the estate to be distributed according to the will of the deceased person. If the deceased didn't make a will then certain rules known as the Laws of Intestacy apply.

Big Issue Lists

To find advice on the first steps to take in the event of a death, enter the words **when someone dies** into your search engine. At the top of the search results in this example was the **Big Issue Lists**. This includes a downloadable document in Adobe PDF format as discussed in Chapter 4 of this book. This document gives a most detailed step-by-step guide to everything that needs to be done to register a death, notify the official authorities and organisations, arrange the funeral, pay any debts and carry out the instructions of any will.

www.bigissuelists.co.uk

The **Association of Retired and People Over 50** site includes instructions on the immediate steps to be taken after a death, such as sending for the doctor, obtaining the death certificate, instructing a funeral director and the possible need for a coroner's post mortem. The donation of organs for medical research is also discussed.

www.arp050.org.uk

Arranging a Funeral

On entering **funerals** into Google, some useful links were immediately found, as discussed below.

The Office of Fair Trading

This is a Government Web site which aims to promote and protect consumer interests throughout the UK, while ensuring that businesses are fair and competitive. The Web site has a section outlining consumers' rights and choices when arranging a funeral. For example, you do not have to have a funeral ceremony, or have a religious minister present. There is a link to the **National Death Centre** which gives information on woodland and green funeral options.

The Office of Fair Trading Web site also gives advice on choosing a funeral director, funeral costs and any financial help that may be available from the Benefits Agency. There is also detailed advice about pre-paid funeral plans and the points that you should consider before joining such a scheme. Finally there is advice for anyone who is dissatisfied with the service given by funeral directors and there are links to two national associations for funeral directors and the **Funeral Standards Council**.

www.oft.gov.uk

UK Funerals On-line

This Web site has a directory of all UK Funeral Directors and Undertakers and there is general advice and information about legal issues. There is also help with bereavement and links to other help organizations. You can obtain online information and pictures of coffins, headstones, etc., and order flowers online. There is also an online facility to order a tree to be planted as a memorial.

www.uk-funerals.co.uk

Probate

It is normal when drawing up a will to appoint one or more *executors*; these are people who will be responsible for distributing the estate when a person dies, according to the wishes expressed in their will. The executors will also be responsible for paying any debts and collecting any money owed to the estate.

Unless the estate is very small, it is necessary to apply for an official legal document authorizing the executors or personal representatives to administer the assets in the estate. For example, a bank or building society may require an official copy (not a photocopy) of the document before allowing the executors to withdraw funds or close an account. If there is no will or no executors are named in a will, beneficiaries of the will or relatives of the deceased may apply for the authority to administer the estate.

The general name for the legal document enabling personal representatives of a deceased person to deal with an estate is a *Grant of Representation*.

- A *Grant of Probate* is issued to one or more executors named in a will.

- *Letters of Administration* are issued when there are no named executors or when executors are unable or unwilling to administer the estate, or when there is no valid will.

The executors or personal representatives must apply to the Probate Registry for a Grant of Probate or Letters of Administration. In the case of a simple estate, obtaining probate and distributing the assets is a straightforward procedure which can be completed without the help of a solicitor.

If the estate is complicated, perhaps involving Inheritance Tax or a contentious will, for example, the services of a qualified solicitor would be advisable. Various application forms and documents must be submitted to the Probate Registry, including a copy of the will and death certificate. An account of the assets in the estate is also needed, including valuation of any property, chattels, savings and investments. Approximate resale values are acceptable and you don't need to employ a professional valuer in the case of a small estate. However, if the total value of the estate is likely to exceed £275,000, additional paperwork will be needed to deal with Inheritance Tax. Before the Grant is issued it is necessary to attend a brief interview at the most convenient regional office of the Probate Registry. A fee is charged for the Grant of Probate and several copies may be needed, to be sent to the various banks, building societies, solicitors, etc., who may be holding assets of the estate.

There is a great deal of help about Probate on the Internet, including explanatory documents and online application forms. A simple search on Google or similar will find lots of firms offering to give advice on Probate. However, if you are applying for a Grant of Probate yourself, or just want to acquaint yourself more with the subject, you should find all the information you need on the **Court Service** Web site, shown below under the link **Wills & Probate**.

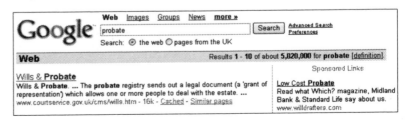

The Court Service

The Court Service is an executive agency of the Government's Department of Constitutional Affairs; its purpose is the delivery of justice in England and Wales. The **Wills & Probate** section of the Court Service Web site has a guide for people applying for probate without a solicitor. All of the information needed is given on the screen, in answer to questions such as, for example, **Why is a grant necessary? Am I entitled to a grant? How do I apply for a grant?** and **Applying for a grant when form IHT200 is needed?** (IHT200 must be completed if Inheritance Tax is due on the estate).

You can also download a copy of the official booklet **PA2, How to obtain probate.** This is in Adobe PDF format as discussed in Chapter 4, so the text can be viewed on the screen or printed on paper.

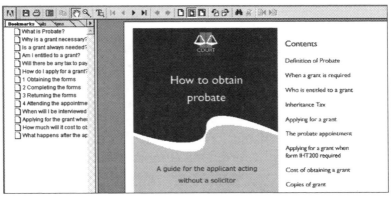

© Crown Copyright

This document is very easy to read and gives a good explanation of the subject for those applying for probate without a solicitor.

The Web site (and booklet PA2) warn that a property cannot be sold until a Grant of Probate has been obtained. However, the Web site also states that banks and building societies sometimes release cash without a grant, if the sums involved are small. The Court Service Web site points out that in the case of an estate which is jointly owned, assets can be passed to the surviving joint owner without the need for a grant of probate.

You can fill in the main **Probate Application Form PA1** online then print it out on paper for posting to the Probate Registry. This form is in the Adobe PDF format as discussed in Chapter 4 of this book.

Form IHT205 and guidance booklet IHT206 enable you to work out if Inheritance Tax is due. These can both be downloaded from the Inland Revenue Web site. Form IHT 205 can be filled in on the screen. Another form, D18 (Probate Summary), must be obtained from the Inland Revenue and completed.

If Inheritance Tax is due because the estate's value exceeds £275,000 (the Nil Rate Band at the time of writing) you are required to fill in a special form, IHT200. However, you are advised to follow the guidance of the Inland Revenue in filling in form IHT200, who may calculate the IHT for you, if you wish. The Inland Revenue will also need to endorse a completed copy of form D18 (Probate Summary). A link to the Inland Revenue Web site is given on the Court Service Web site. To complete the application for a Grant of Probate, forms PA1, IHT205 (but not IHT200) and D18 must be returned to the Probate Registry.

www.courtservice.gov.uk

www.inlandrevenue.gov.uk

10

Healthy Living

Introduction

A recent survey suggested that health issues rather than money are the biggest worry as people get older. This chapter looks at some of the many Web sites giving advice on healthy living, including topics such as diet and nutrition, exercise and the use of the Internet to find information and help for specific illnesses.

Of course, sensible eating, moderation in alcohol intake, giving up smoking, avoiding obesity and keeping fit are desirable objectives for people of all ages; in later life it is necessary to try even harder to stay fit and active. Older people are less likely to be rushing about in a career, raising children or playing active sports, which all burn off the calories; for older people who are retired there may be more time for leisurely pub lunches and to enjoy the odd beer or glass or two of wine.

Common problems of ageing such as arthritic joints may also make it difficult to maintain physical fitness. On the positive side, many older people have more time for healthy exercise such as walking and swimming; also time to eat sensibly rather than grabbing "junk" food and eating "on the hoof" like many younger people.

There are many Web sites aimed at keeping the older generation fitter for longer; some examples are given on the next few pages.

Sixtyplusurfers is an online magazine for "senior citizens". It has help and advice on all aspects of life for older people and includes sections devoted to **Health and Fitness**, **Personal Health**, **Healthy Eating** and **Staying Fit**.

www.sixtyplusurfers.co.uk

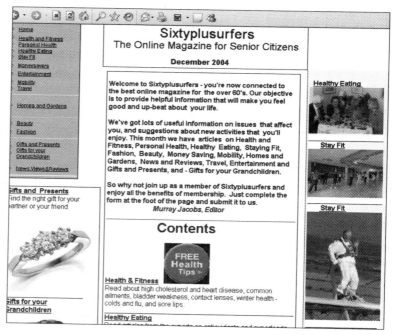

Clicking on the **Health and Fitness** link on the above Web page causes a number of articles to be displayed including advice on **High Cholesterol**. There are also

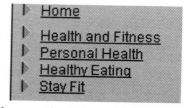

articles on a multifocus contact lens and colds and 'flu.

The **Personal Health** section of the Sixtyplusurfers site is described as "**The page for that embarrassing problem**". These include prostate problems affecting, it is stated, 50% of men over 50, amounting to 8 million sufferers in the UK. The site recommends some commercial products for prostate and also haemorrhoid problems.

Clicking the **Healthy Eating** link on the **Sixtyplusurfers** site presents an article on **Antioxidants and the Superfoods**. This article explains that Superfoods have health-enhancing properties and includes a list of 20 of the best available. These are mainly fruit, nuts and vegetables, some of which, it is stated, reduce the risk of cancer.

The **Stay Fit** section of the **Sixtyplusurfers** site includes an "**AGE REDUCTION PLAN**". This presents a list of steps to lower your blood pressure, such as reducing your intake of fat, alcohol and salt combined with more exercise and reduced weight. **Action Plans** are given for reducing cholesterol and also programmes of exercise. You are advised to consult your doctor and a certified personal trainer or fitness consultant before starting a fitness programme.

The **Stay Fit** section of the **Sixtyplusurfers** site also has an article on **BMI**, the **Body Mass Index** used to find out if you are the correct weight for your height or overweight, obese or morbidly obese. There is a link to an online BMI calculator and there are lots more of these on the Internet. You can find these by entering the words **Body Mass Index** into your search engine. (BMI will find a well-known airline!). BMI is discussed in more detail later in this chapter.

Diets and Health

The British Nutrition Foundation is a charitable organization funded by the government, the food industry and other sources.

www.nutrition.org.uk

The BNF site is very well laid out and easy to use. Clicking **Information** as shown on the extract below presents a menu which includes a further menu **Nutrition through life**. As shown below, one of the options is **Older Adults**. This page recommends, for example, that people over 65 should take a vitamin D supplement, eat oily fish and engage in regular physical activity to maintain mobility.

This Web page also recommends that older people increase their intake of fibre, fruit and vegetables. Foods such as these can, it is stated, benefit conditions such as cataracts, heart disease and osteoporosis.

Diet-i.com is a Web site compiled by a team of researchers and includes a lot of material on diets for older people. The site lists many UK and American organizations as its references, including the US Department of Agriculture, the UK Health Service, the American Dietetic Association and the British Heart Foundation.

www.diet-i.com

The **Diet-i.com** site stresses the desirability of a high fibre diet, including lots of fruit and vegetables together with plenty of fluids. The site points out that the calorie needs of people decreases in later years and there is a table of average calorie needs for different age groups.

Elderly People and Calorie Needs

As we age, our calorie needs decrease due to a drop in muscle strength from taking less physical activity. However, vitamin and mineral needs may stay the same or even increase if the body absorbs them less efficiently.

Average Calorie Needs Throughout Life

Age Group		1-3	4-6	7-10	11-14	15-18	19-59	60-74	75+
Calorie Needs	Male	1230	1715	1970	2220	2755	2550	2350	2100
Calorie Needs	Female	1165	1545	1740	1845	2110	1940	1900	1810

Note: These are average values only. Heavier or more active people may need more.

Foods to Include for Optimum Health

Fruit
In particular those high in Vitamin C, like blackberries, strawberries, raspberries, blackcurrants, citrus fruit, kiwi fruit, peaches, mango, cantaloupe melon, apples.

The **Diet-i.com** site also includes lists of **Foods to Include for Optimum Health** and **Foods to Avoid for Optimum Seniors Health**. Sample diets are included.

The Blueberry

Berries of various types, such as blackberries, strawberries, raspberries, blackcurrants, etc., are widely recommended as part of a healthy diet. The real star, however, is the blueberry, with at least one Web site devoted to its health benefits.

www.wildblueberries.com

The above Web site quotes research from the US Department of Agriculture ranking the blueberry higher than cranberries, strawberries, prunes and raspberries for its antioxidant capacity. This is its ability to protect against diseases like cancer, heart disease and Alzheimer's as well as fighting vision problems and the effects of ageing. Their high vitamin C content is also good for bladder problems and cystitis.

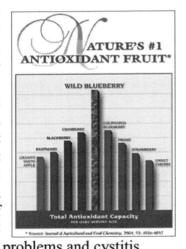

English blueberries are available in season from some large supermarkets and from **The Dorset Blueberry Company**. Their Web site has an online shop for the ordering of blueberry-related products, a blueberry recipe archive and articles on the history and health benefits of blueberries (also known as bilberries).

www.dorset-blueberry.com

The Web site for **Help the Aged** recommends that older people eat more nutritionally dense foods (but in smaller servings) such as fruit and vegetables, wholemeal bread and cereals, fish and meat and milk and dairy foods. There are articles on anti-ageing and the benefits of eating "five portions" of fruit and vegetables a day.

www.helptheaged.org.uk

The CenNet site for over-50s covers a wide range of lifestyle topics including a section on eating for health.

www.cennet.co.uk

The **SilverSurfers** site has links to Web sites on most subjects of interest to older people, including the extract below which is found by following the thread **SilverSurfers - Health & Fitness - Dieting & Nutrition**.

www.silversurfers.net

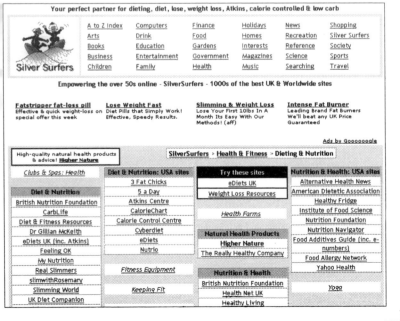

The **WeightWatchers** site, for people of all ages, has a lot of articles on diet, recipes, exercise and fitness, including an online Body Mass Index calculator, as discussed earlier in this chapter. If you wish to lose weight by attending WeightWatchers you can find a meeting near your home by entering your postcode online.

www.weightwatchers.co.uk

Meetings are our best way to lose weight

For over 40 years, Weight Watchers has helped millions of people around the world to lose weight.

Find a Meeting
Enter postcode
Learn More

Can't go to Meetings? Try Weight Watchers Online
Follow **Time To Eat** online with our unbeatable weight-loss tools and resources.

Sign up now | Learn More

If you can't attend WeightWatchers meetings for any reason there is an online programme which helps you to monitor what you eat, within a maximum daily **POINTS** total. Click <u>Learn More</u> as shown at the bottom right above for more information.

The **BUPA** Web site contains a section on **Diet and Nutrition**. There are lots of questions aimed at analysing your food and exercise habits, followed by very comprehensive advice on healthy eating and nutrition.

www.bupa.co.uk

The **Food Standards Agency** is an independent food safety watchdog set up by the government to protect the public's health. There are two easy-to-use Web sites giving very thorough information on healthy diets and nutrition, including an **Older people** page.

www.food.gov.uk   **www.eatwell.gov.uk**

Fitness and Exercise

There are many Web sites giving fitness programmes for older people. It is generally stressed that anyone planning to start such a programme should first consult their GP. This is particularly important for anyone suffering from any sort of medical condition.

The **Seniors Network** Web site outlines the benefits of being more active, including strengthening your heart, lowering blood pressure, etc., and thus enabling you to **"Gain the passport to ripe old age..."**. Tips are given for making a habit of activities such as walking, swimming, cycling, running and jogging. Fitness assessment is also discussed and in particular criteria such as blood pressure, cholesterol, percentage body fat, strength, stamina, suppleness and aerobic capacity.

The Seniors Network site also discusses **Strength Training for Seniors** to replace some of the muscle strength lost by the ageing process.

www.seniorsnetwork.co.uk

The **Sixtyplusurfers Online Magazine** includes an action plan to increase your strength. Depending on your health (and after first consulting your doctor) you might do strength-building exercises in the gym or cardiovascular activity such as walking or running. The Sixtyplusurfers Web site states that the maximum **Age Reduction** benefit occurs when 1000 to 3,500 calories are expended a week.

www.sixtyplusurfers.co.uk

Later Life Training is an organization which runs courses for trainers in **Exercise for the Prevention of Falls & Injuries in Frailer Older People**. These are intended to increase the safety, independence and quality of life of older people.

www.laterlifetraining.co.uk

Later Life Training is staffed by people with experience and qualifications in health issues for older people including prevention of falls, osteoporosis and research into ageing and physical activity.

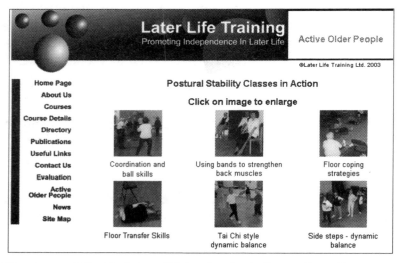

The **Later Life Training** Web site includes a list of **Useful Links** such as the **Register of Exercise Professionals** who specialize in activities such as gym instruction, yoga, keep fit and personal training. There are links to Web sites from major charities offering leaflets on topics such as exercise, falls prevention and keeping fit. There are also links to books and videos on exercise for older people and details of exercise courses in different parts of the country.

The **Excite UK** directory has links to over 30 Web sites providing information on all aspects of fitness and exercise for people over 50.   There are sites providing equipment such as **Multi Gyms** and videos and DVDs on **Salsa Dancing** and instruction in **T'ai Chi**. The **Excite Directory** can be viewed at:

www.excite.co.uk

Once on the Excite Web site follow the thread shown below.

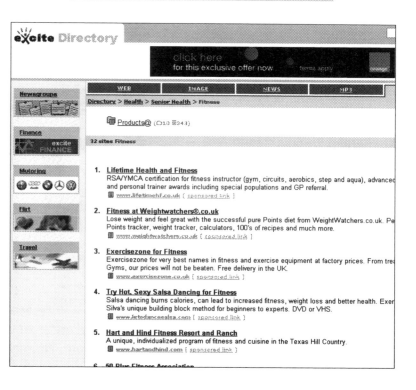

Body Mass Index (BMI)

This is a figure calculated from your height and weight. The results of the calculation may suggest that you are underweight, overweight or obese. You can easily find your BMI, after entering the words **body mass index** into a search engine such as Google. Lots of free BMI calculators appear in the results such as the one shown below from the American **NHLBI**. Simply enter your height and weight and click **Compute BMI**, as shown below. There are tabs to allow you to use **STANDARD** (Imperial Units – feet, inches, etc.) or **METRIC**.

www.nhlbisupport.com

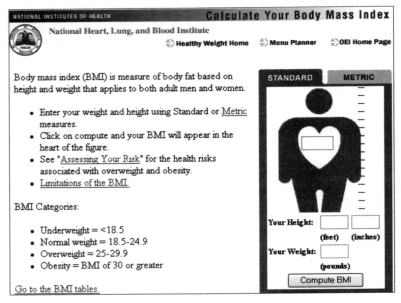

After calculating your **BMI**, the small table above under **BMI Categories** indicates whether you are **Underweight, Normal weight, Overweight** or suffering from **Obesity**.

Measuring Your Own Blood Pressure

Blood pressure is not just a measure of your level of general fitness; high blood pressure affects millions of people in Britain and is a major cause of serious illnesses such as heart attacks and strokes. High blood pressure (also known as hypertension) often goes undetected since there are no obvious symptoms. Ideally high blood pressure can be reduced by a healthy lifestyle, including weight loss, exercise, a sensible diet, giving up smoking and low alcohol consumption. Failing that, many people now have their high blood pressure brought under control by medication.

Enter **monitoring blood pressure** into your search engine to find lots of articles on the subject. **NetDoctor.co.uk** is a wide-ranging medical Web site which includes a comprehensive article, written and reviewed by doctors, describing the measurement of blood pressure.

www.netdoctor.co.uk

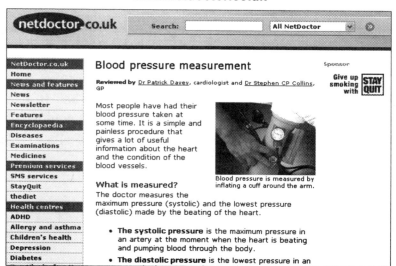

Some people suffer from what doctors call the "white coat syndrome". Their blood pressure rises due to anxiety when their B.P. is being measured in the medical centre. In such cases the doctor may recommend that the patient obtains a personal B.P. monitor and takes readings in the (theoretically) more relaxed environment at home. The search mentioned on the previous page will find, in the results, links to numerous companies offering personal blood pressure monitors. These links appear on the right-hand side of the Web page under **Sponsored Links**, as shown here on the right.

If your GP agrees that it's a good idea to monitor your B.P., they may be able to recommend an approved make.

The **monitoring blood pressure** search mentioned previously also includes links to reputable professional and charitable organizations such as the **British Heart Foundation** and the **British Hypertension Society**. These include useful, high quality articles and information about high blood pressure. The British Hypertension Society also lists B.P. monitoring equipment which has been tested and validated for home use.

Sponsored Links

Blood Pressure Monitors
Massive Sale Now On. **Blood Pressure** Monitors. Cheap Prices. Fast UK Del
www.physiosupplies.com

UK **Blood Pressure** Monitor
Huge Range of Brands (aff)
Cheap, Easy to Use, Fast Delivery
www.2004deals.com

Blood Pressure Monitors
High quality at low prices.
Selected and approved by BUPA
www.bupa-shop.co.uk

www.bhf.org.uk

www.hyp.ac.uk

Please note that you should always consult your doctor for advice on any matter concerning your health or fitness.

Cutting Down on Alcohol

Alcohol can be a great source of pleasure for many older people and when taken in moderation can be both healthy and relaxing. Unfortunately excessive drinking can have a number of harmful consequences including damage to health, increased risk of injury through accidents, etc., and psychiatric disorder. The following are generally stated as maximum safe limits for alcohol consumption:

No more than 3-4 units daily for a man.

No more than 2-3 units daily for a woman.

(1 unit of alcohol is a half-pint of ordinary beer or lager, a small glass of wine (9% alcohol by volume) or a single pub measure of spirits.)

Alcoholics Anonymous

Anyone drinking more than these limits may wish to consider cutting down on their alcohol consumption. For anyone seriously worried about their drinking or that of a friend or relative, Alcoholics Anonymous is probably the most well-known source of help.

www.alcoholics-anonymous.org.uk

The Alcoholics Anonymous Web site gives a telephone number which is staffed 24 hours a day and is completely confidential. Alcoholics Anonymous can also be contacted by e-mail. There are articles about alcoholism and lists of **Frequently Asked Questions. Local A.A. Web Pages** gives the days, times and venues of meetings in different parts of the country.

Alcohol Concern is a national voluntary agency and provides a great deal of information and services for people with alcohol-related problems. It is a registered charity.

www.alcoholconcern.org.uk

Alcohol Concern produces a large number of press releases and reports (many in Adobe PDF format as discussed in Chapter 4 of this book). These cover many aspects of alcohol misuse including "binge drinking", drink driving, and anxiety disorders. There is an online **Bookshop & Library**, including a leaflet I **don't mind if I do ...Alcohol and older people... safer drinking for the over 60s.**

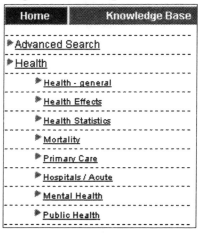

The **NHS Direct** Web site has a section on **Alcohol Misuse**.

www.nhsdirect.nhs.uk

This site has advice on problem levels of drinking, telephone numbers for help and advice on treatment. There are links to sites giving help on alcohol-related problems.

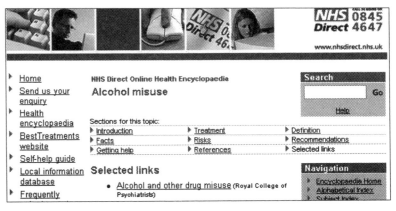

© Crown Copyright

Down Your Drink is a Web site run by Alcohol Concern and partly funded by the Department of Health. The Web site lists the benefits of cutting down on alcohol and there are questions to determine if someone has a drink problem. There is also a free, confidential, 6-week course involving 1 hour a week online, to help people reduce their drinking.

www.downyourdrink.org.uk

The Portman Group represents the main suppliers and retailers of alcohol in this country. Its stated purpose is to tackle the social problems caused by alcohol misuse. It has a **Code of Practice** which is intended to encourage the sensible marketing of alcohol by the large suppliers.

www.portmangroup.org.uk

Giving Up Smoking

At the time of writing there is much controversy about smoking bans in places where food is served. It is claimed that smoking kills 120,000 people a year in Britain and that 364,000 people are taken to hospital with smoking-related illnesses. There are several organizations with Internet Web sites aimed at helping people to stop smoking.

ASH (Action on Smoking and Health (UK)) has a lot of articles aimed at helping people to quit. There are links to other Web sites, such as **QUIT**, with examples of people who have succeeded in stopping smoking. The ASH site also lists a very large number of downloadable booklets and leaflets on smoking issues. These are in Adobe Acrobat format as discussed in Chapter 4 of this book.

The **British Heart Foundation** is behind several successful advertising campaigns for people to stop smoking and there is a BHF smoking mini Web site. There are tips to help people to give up and a feature to help you find professionals and groups in your area, after entering your postcode online. There are also ready-made warning signs which you can print out and put on someone's cigarette packet. Standard e-mail messages are available to be sent to someone to encourage them to stop smoking.

www.bhf.org.uk/smoking

The **Click2Quit** site includes advice on how to stop smoking, personal stories and a **Click2Quit Programme**, a plan to stop smoking using patches, lozenges and gums.

www.click2quit.com

Finding Out About Illnesses

This book most emphatically does not recommend that anyone should try to use the Internet to diagnose their own illness. Amateur self-diagnosis using the Internet may reach mistaken conclusions and cause great anxiety and unnecessary suffering. Anyone worried about any sort of medical problem should consult their GP and obtain help from qualified medical professionals.

However, if someone has been professionally diagnosed with a specific illness and wants to find out more information, the Internet has a huge amount of information provided by ethical organizations. GPs themselves are often under tremendous pressure with thousands of patients on their list and may not have the time to discuss an illness at great length. The Internet can supplement the advice given by the medical professionals and provide additional background information collected from an enormous pool of experts worldwide. Looking at such information provided by medical bodies, academic institutions and charities can help people to understand a particular illness and may help them to cope better. For some illnesses there will also be support groups with whom you can have an online discussion and obtain help and advice.

In general, all you need to do is to enter the name of an illness or disease into a search engine such as Google, as shown below. For example, we could try to find out about arthritis, which affects so many older people. A total of 8,000,000 people of all ages suffer from arthritis in the UK.

On clicking **Search** the Internet returns a staggering 1,040,000 results linking to Web sites containing the word **arthritis**.

Results **1 - 10** of about **1,040,000** for **arthritis** [definition]. **(0.26** seconds

This was a search confined to the UK - a worldwide search yields 12,300,000 results. (Don't worry, you'll probably find all you need on the first couple of pages, since the most relevant and frequently visited Web sites are listed first in the results).

As shown by the first page of results below, the links listed down the left-hand side lead to various charities and other organizations providing information and help on arthritis.

Arthritis Research & Therapy |
news. Latest news. Blood Filter Treatment Safe for Severe **Arthritis** [10 December 2004] Being Thin Has Downside for People with **Arthritis** [9 December 2004] Unlike ...
arthritis-research.com/ - 32k - 11 Dec 2004 - Cached - Similar pages

   Arthritis Research & Therapy |
   news. Latest news. Long-Term NSAIDs May Not Be Useful for Osteoarthritis [30 N 2004] Work Environment Tied to **Arthritis** Disability Risk [30 November 2004 ...
   arthritis-research.com/home/ - 30k - Cached - Similar pages
   [More results from arthritis-research.com]

Arthritis Research Campaign
The **Arthritis** Research Campaign (ARC), founded in 1936, raises funds to promote medical research into the cause, treatment and cure of arthritic conditions: to ...
www.arc.org.uk/ - 30k - 11 Dec 2004 - Cached - Similar pages

   Arthritis Research Campaign | Diet and **Arthritis**
   There is a lot of confusing advice on diet in magazines and books, and many food supplements which are claimed to help with **arthritis**. ...
   www.arc.org.uk/about_arth/booklets/6010/6010.htm - 59k - 11 Dec 2004 - Cached
   [More results from www.arc.org.uk]

arthritiscare.org.uk/UK - empowering people with **arthritis**
... **Arthritis** Care - empowering people with **arthritis**. Christmas is fast approaching, so why not buy your Christmas cards and gifts from **Arthritis** Care. ...
www.**arthritis**care.org.uk/ - 15k - Cached - Similar pages

BBC - Health - Conditions - The **arthritis** guide
... The **arthritis** guide. **Arthritis** is a common condition that affects an estimated 8 million people in the UK. ... In The **arthritis** guide. Clasped hands About **arthritis**. ...
www.bbc.co.uk/health/conditions/**arthritis**/ - 42k - 11 Dec 2004 - Cached - Similar pages

The **Sponsored Links** on the right-hand side are links to the Web sites of commercial companies who have paid to advertise their products or services on Google.

One of the results in the previous search is the **Netdoctor.co.uk** Web site, which includes an online article about arthritis, as shown below. There is also a link to a list of medicines used to treat arthritis.

Sponsored Links

Need relief from pain?
The healthy way to conquer pain without drugs - Acticare TSE
www.acticare.com

Which? Online review
Unbiased **arthritis** advice
And 100s more consumer topics
trial.which.co.uk/

Overcome Joint Pain
MicroLactin a clinically proven aid
Innovative supplement for **arthritis**
www.Microlactin.info

www.netdoctor.co.uk

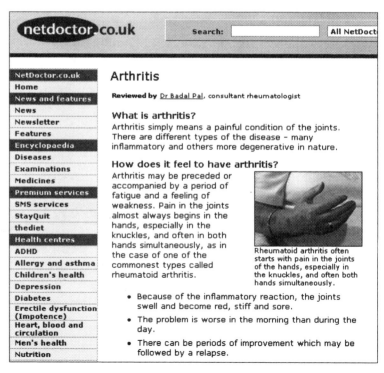

netdoctor.co.uk   Search: All NetDoct

NetDoctor.co.uk
Home
News and features
News
Newsletter
Features
Encyclopaedia
Diseases
Examinations
Medicines
Premium services
SMS services
StayQuit
thediet
Health centres
ADHD
Allergy and asthma
Children's health
Depression
Diabetes
Erectile dysfunction (Impotence)
Heart, blood and circulation
Men's health
Nutrition

Arthritis

Reviewed by Dr Badal Pal, consultant rheumatologist

What is arthritis?
Arthritis simply means a painful condition of the joints. There are different types of the disease – many inflammatory and others more degenerative in nature.

How does it feel to have arthritis?
Arthritis may be preceded or accompanied by a period of fatigue and a feeling of weakness. Pain in the joints almost always begins in the hands, especially in the knuckles, and often in both hands simultaneously, as in the case of one of the commonest types called rheumatoid arthritis.

Rheumatoid arthritis often starts with pain in the joints of the hands, especially in the knuckles, and often both hands simultaneously.

- Because of the inflammatory reaction, the joints swell and become red, stiff and sore.
- The problem is worse in the morning than during the day.
- There can be periods of improvement which may be followed by a relapse.

Department of Health

The Department of Health Web site has a section devoted to the care of older people, primarily for NHS organizations and local councils but also of interest to older people and carers.

www.dh.gov.uk

Select **Policy and guidance, Health and social care topics** and **Older people's services**. You can download a report to the Government, **Better Health in Old Age**, in Adobe Acrobat PDF format (as discussed in Chapter 4). There are numerous other reports and information on health for older people and a list of **Older people's services useful links**.

NHS Direct

This is the online part of the telephone emergency service which you can call if you are feeling unwell. The emergency telephone number is given onscreen, enabling you to speak to a nurse at any time of the day or night. There is a self-help guide online, a definition of an emergency and an online health encyclopaedia.

www.nhsdirect.nhs.uk

© Crown Copyright

The NHS Gateway

This NHS site includes a new feature **NHS Search** which enables over 600,000 NHS documents to be searched by entering a keyword or phrase in the **Search the NHS** bar.

www.nhs.uk

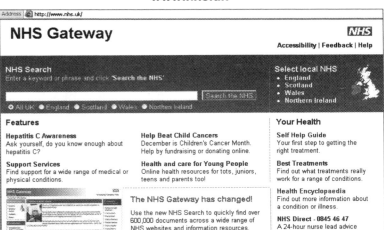

© Crown Copyright

As shown above on the right, there are also links to the **NHS Direct** facilities discussed previously, i.e. the **Self Help Guide**, **Best Treatments** for various conditions and the telephone number to dial for help and advice from **NHS Direct**. (Also the **NHS 24** telephone number for Scotland.)

Surgerydoor

This is a health Web site providing information on a wide range of subjects with articles on, for example, **Diseases in Depth**, **Healthy Living** and **Complementary Medicine**, and there is also an online **Medical Dictionary**.

www.surgerydoor.co.uk

Ask-The-Doc

This site allows you to e-mail your symptoms to a doctor and, (for a fee), receive a reply. There is a note pointing out that the reply is not a medical diagnosis and that you should consult your doctor for any medical problems.

www.ask-the-doc.com

healthsites

This Web site is a *portal*, i.e. it provides links to many other UK health Web sites and some overseas. These sites cover specific diseases, specialist advice, fact sheets, support groups and complementary medicine, for example.

www.healthsites.co.uk

CenNet

CenNet provides general advice for the over 50s and includes a feature **Medical Links**, enabling you to connect to sites offering advice on specific illnesses, including a mental health section. Another link, **Alternative Medicines**, connects to sites covering, for example, **Acupuncture**, **Pilates, Homeopathy, Hypnosis, Reflexology** and **Tai Chai**.

www.cennet.co.uk

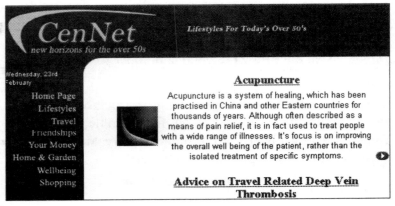

Help and Support

Introduction

There are currently19.8 million people aged 50 and over in the UK population and the number is expected to continue rising. 7 in 10 women aged over 85 now live alone. (You can find these and other statistics on the Government Web site **www.statistics.gov.uk**. Select **Older People** from the drop-down menu under the heading **FOCUS ON**.) At the same time, the number of beds available in nursing homes, etc., for older and physically disabled people has declined sharply. So in the future many older people are going to need help to enable them to stay in their own homes.

Many people would prefer to stay in their own home as long as possible, perhaps with the company of a beloved pet and surrounded by family photographs and a lifetime's memories. However, even the most fit and independent of people may find living at home a struggle as they get older; everyday tasks such as shopping, driving, cooking, cleaning and bathing may become very difficult. Outside help may be essential if an older person is to continue living in their home.

This chapter looks at some of the Web sites providing advice and support for older people, including those with disabilities.

If you enter some relevant keywords, such as **support older disabled people**, into a search engine like Google, you will get an idea of the sort of organizations providing services.

A shown below, many of these sites are provided by charities, the government and local authorities.

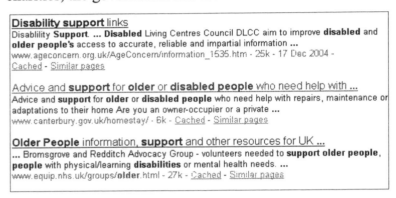

For example, the **Homestay Agency** page on the **Canterbury City Council** Web site listed above offers advice and support for older or disabled people who need help with repairs, maintenance or adaptations to their home. This includes visits to the person's home to give advice, get estimates from reliable tradesmen, help to obtain grants and loans and provide support until the work is completed. The Homestay Agency also offers to review a disabled person's housing circumstances and help with any essential adaptations to the building.

Another of the results shown on the previous page is a link to an NHS site called **EQUIP** – **Electronic Quality Information for Patients**. This includes **Support Contacts for Older People** in the form of lists of Internet links. There are two lists, **National contacts** and **West Midlands health contacts**.

EQUI☺P   **Support Contacts for Older People**

Home	There are pages of information on <u>specific medical conditions</u>, <u>bereavement</u>, <u>disability support</u>, <u>services</u> that might affect older people and this page is for more general support.
Information Topics	
General Health Information	**National contacts** **West Midlands health contacts**
Further information	**National contacts:**
Search	• <u>Action on Elder Abuse</u>, Astral House, 1268 London Road, London SW16 4ER Tel: 020 8 Email: <u>enquiries@elderabuse.org.uk</u>
Other languages	• <u>Active for Life</u>, Tel: 01179 406 409 - a falls prevention programme • <u>Age Concern England</u>, 1268 London Road, London SW16 4ER Information Line: 0800 00 provides practical help, information and advice
Disclaimer	• <u>Anchor Trust</u> - not-for-profit provider of housing, care and support for older people in Engl • <u>Bereavement support</u> on EQUIP • Canine Concern - dogs visiting homes and hospitals for the sick, lonely and elderly Tel: 0 • <u>Care Homes</u> - searchable list of residential and nursing homes in UK • <u>Care UK Net</u> - provides a selection of useful links with detailed descriptions • <u>Caring Decisions</u> - Tel: 020 7402 2702 Email: <u>cdecisions@dial.pipex.com</u> provides infor and care receivers make informed decisions specific to long term care, with a special s • Cinnamon Trust, Foundry House, Foundry Square, Hayle, Cornwall TR27 4HE Tel: 0173 elderly and terminally ill people and their pets. • <u>Contact the Elderly</u>, 15 Henrietta Street, Covent Garden, London WC2E 8QG Tel: 0207 Email: <u>info@contact-the-elderly.org</u> A national charity providing volunteer support for olde • <u>Counsel and Care</u> - Twyman House, 16 Bonny Street, London NW1 9PG Tel: 0207 241 8 <u>advice@counselandcare.org.uk</u> Helpline: 0845 300 7585 Mon-Fri 10am-1pm Advice for p families • <u>Elderly Accommodation Counsel</u>, 3rd Floor, 89 Albert Embankment, London SE1 7TP T

© Crown Copyright

The above links cover a wide range of support topics for older people, including links to the main charities like **Age Concern**, lists of residential care homes and support for carers. There is also a link to the **Home Safety Network**, provided by the Department of Trade and Industry.

Another link in the list above opens up the Web site of the **Home Improvement Agencies**. These are locally based, not-for-profit organizations whose aim is to assist vulnerable older or disabled homeowners and tenants.

Help from Local Authorities

The main provider of many of the services for people needing support is the local authority, such as your town, city, borough or county council. You can find out about the range of services offered by entering the name of the council into your search engine. Then you should be able to look at the relevant department, such as Social Services or Social Care, etc. Here you will find articles outlining the services and giving useful contact telephone numbers.

For example, if you wish to have your home adapted with certain mobility aids, your needs will have to be assessed. There may also be means testing to determine what level of financial support may be given. You will probably be able to "download" and print out PDF documents giving further information. PDF documents are discussed in Chapter 4. In some cases, such as the Blue Badge disabled parking scheme, the application form can be completed on the screen or downloaded then printed and filled in manually.

Local authorities may be able to help with the following:

- "Meals on wheels"
- Home maintenance
- Home security
- Adapted housing for disabled people
- Specialist equipment such as wheelchairs, etc.
- Sheltered housing
- Day care
- Blue Badge parking scheme for disabled people
- Support for carers
- Benefits for older people.

In the example below, Leicestershire County Council was chosen at random and entered into Google.

After clicking the **Search** button shown above, a list of results appeared with the official Web site of Leicestershire County Council at the top, as shown below.

On clicking the link **Leicester County Council's website** shown above the home page opens up as shown on the next page.

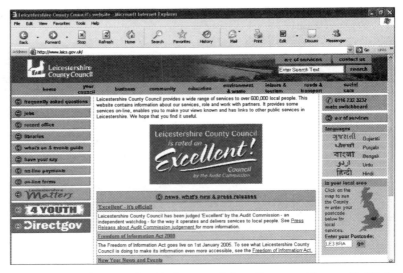

As shown above, the Leicestershire County Council Web site home page has links to all of the various services, such as jobs, on-line payments and forms. Across the top of the Web page, the different themed areas are listed, including **social care**, as shown in the extract below.

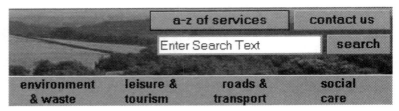

There is also an opportunity to search for information within the Leicestershire site. This is done by entering your own keywords to replace **Enter Search Text** as shown above. Then click the **search** button to begin looking for information on your chosen topic.

For example, entering **Stilton Cheese** finds links to 19 articles referring to the famous Leicestershire product.

There is also an **a-z of services** button, as shown below, which leads to various listings such as those shown below under the letter **A**.

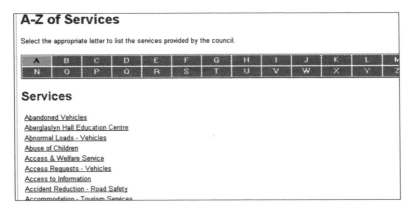

These include, for example, **Activities for Older People, Assessment For Adaptations to the Home,** and **Assessing an Adult Who is Blind or Partially Sighted**.

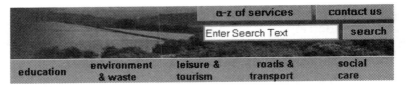

The **social care** button is shown above on the right of the Leicestershire County Council home page. Click this link to see the full range of Social Services, as shown below.

When you select **Older People** as shown on the left above, you are presented with a choice of links to services for older people, such as those shown in the extract on the right below.

For example, **Adaptations** gives details of help with improvements to enable an elderly or disabled person to cope in their own home. This includes grants to help with the installation of equipment such as grab rails, stair rails and larger items such as showers and stairlifts.

Older People

- Eligibility Criteria
- Home Care
- Day Care
- Adaptations
- Disabled Persons' Parking
- Adult Placement Service

Charities and Other Organisations

Leonard Cheshire

Leonard Cheshire is one of the leading charities in the UK and also operates in 57 countries worldwide. Leonard Cheshire provides residential/nursing care in 85 homes across the UK. The charity also helps 7000 disabled people in the UK to continue to live independently in their own homes. Support may vary from a care worker visiting for a few hours a week to respite care in which staff live in for up to two weeks. The Leonard Cheshire charity also provides holidays for disabled people and their carers at The Park House Hotel on the Sandringham Estate in Norfolk.

www.leonard-cheshire.org

Please also see: **www.lc-uk.org**

IndependentAge

This is the Royal United Kingdom Beneficent Association, a national charity that champions independence for older people. IndependentAge has residential and nursing homes as well as providing extra income, support and friendship. The charity relies on donations and volunteers and the Web site has details of fundraising events such as the **Trek Peru 2005**. IndependentAge helps people over 65 (or over 40 if they are disabled) who have a low income. The Web site enables you to order a free copy of the guide **60-Wise!**

- Financial grants and benefits
- Safety and Security at home
- Coping with Confusion
- Keeping your affairs shipshape
- Moving into suitable accommodation
- Residential and nursing care
- Charities and organisations providing help

Another free guide, **60-Wise at Home**, can also be ordered online from the IndependentAge Web site.

- Around the house
- Relaxing in your living room
- Cooking and eating
- Comfort in your bedroom
- Independence in the bathroom
- Making the most of your garden
- Obtaining advice and products

www.independentage.org.uk

Help the Aged

This is one of the leading charities working with older people in Britain. The stated priorities of Help the Aged include combating poverty, reducing loneliness, defeating negative ideas about age and making sure older people receive good care. The Web site gives information on the services available such as the provision of vehicles to help older people get out and about. There are 35 **Handyvans** around the country, used by Help the Aged to help people feel safe at home by fitting devices such as door chains, window locks and smoke detectors. Gardening help is also provided by Help the Aged. The Web site includes information on **Food & Fitness, Community** and **Money Matters**, for example, and there is a section covering **Campaigns and News**. On the left-hand side of the Help the Aged Web site, the link **Text too small** explains how to set up your computer to make the screen easier to read.

www.helptheaged.org.uk

Age Concern

Age Concern supports all people over 50 in the UK, and aims "to ensure that they get the most from life." The Age Concern Web site lists their essential products and services including providing access to Computers and IT. There is also information and factsheets about the complete range of topics which concern older people, such as caring and benefits, money and finance, leisure and learning, health, housing and running your home. Discussion boards allow you to join online conversations about all sorts of topics. Alternatively you can start your own discussion if none of the current subjects appeals to you.

www.ace.org.uk

Help With Disabilities

Foundations

This is the National Co-ordinating Body for Home Improvement Agencies (HIAs) in England. The HIAs are not-for-profit locally-based organizations which help older, disabled or low income homeowners or private sector tenants to repair, maintain or adapt their home. This Web site, supported by the Office of the Deputy Prime Minister, incorporates a number of accessibility features to make it easier to read. The Web site includes many pages relevant to disabled older people such as an article on Disabled Facilities Grants (DFGs) used to finance adaptations. These are available from local authorities and can be worth £25,000 or more. The Foundations site also includes documents in Adobe PDF format, which can be downloaded and printed, as discussed in Chapter 4.

www.cel.co.uk/foundations

The Disabled Living Centres Council

This organization provides a UK network of centres which give advice and the opportunity to try out the complete range of equipment for people with special needs, as shown on the Web site extract on the next page. The Disabled Living Centres Council page states that the advice you receive "is always impartial because, by and large, centres don't sell equipment." There are maps to help you find your nearest Disabled Living Centre using your county or postcode, etc. A list of the Disabled Living Centres in Adobe PDF format can be downloaded and printed from this Web site, as discussed in Chapter 4.

www.dlcc.org.uk

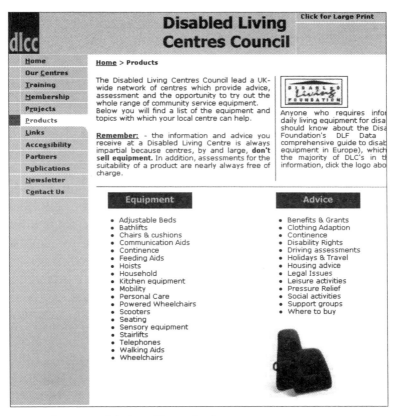

The Disabled Living Foundation

The Disabled Living Centres use a database of disability equipment provided by the **Disabled Living Foundation**. This database is available in 3 formats – print, CD-ROM and Internet. Information on the Disabled Living Foundation can be viewed by clicking the link shown at the top right of the DLCC page above.

www.dlf.org.uk

The British Council of Disabled People (BCODP)

This is the UK's national organization of the worldwide Disabled People's Movement. It was set up in 1981 to promote equality and participation for disabled people in UK society. Non-disabled people can join as Supporting Members. There are currently 126 groups run by disabled people in the UK. The Web site includes a job finding service for disabled people and a customer finding service for self-employed disabled people.

The BCODP Web site also includes articles on a wide range of relevant topics such as Disability Law and Disability Discrimination. There are also online forums for the discussion of topics such as the Disability Living Allowance and accessibility issues for disabled users of Web sites. A regular online newsletter is produced, downloadable in Adobe PDF format and there are also audio versions. The newsletter requires Adobe Acrobat Reader to be installed on your computer as discussed in Chapter 4 of this book. The BCODP Web site includes a link to download the free Acrobat Reader to your computer.

Get Acrobat Reader

www.bcodp.org.uk

RNIB -The Royal National Institute of the Blind

This is the leading UK charity offering support and advice to over 2 million people with sight problems. Apart from help with Braille, Talking Books, computer training and solutions to many everyday problems, RNIB also funds research into the prevention and treatment of eye disease and fights for equal rights for people with sight problems.

www.rnib.org.uk

Glasses and Contact Lenses

There are now many firms offering discount glasses and contact lenses, which can be ordered online. First you obtain a prescription from a local optician, from whom you are not legally obliged to buy your glasses. You are entitled to free eye tests and prescriptions if you are over 60 or on income support or other benefits. You may also be able to get an **NHS optical voucher** for help with the cost of the glasses or contact lenses. For more information on free eye tests and other help, have a look at the Citizen's Advice Bureau site at the Web address shown below:

www.adviceguide.org.uk

A search on Google or similar using key words such as **prescription glasses**, for example, will find a number of companies offering glasses at discount prices.

The **GLASSESDIRECT.CO.UK** Web site has a Frequently Asked Questions (FAQ) feature which explains the whole ordering process. For example, certain essential dimensions can be read off an existing pair of glasses with the aid of a magnifying glass.

www.glassesdirect.co.uk

The Deafblind Web Site

This Web site contains a lot of information of interest to anyone who is deaf, blind or both and also for those who would like to help people with these disabilities. An important feature of the site is the **Deafblind Manual Alphabet**, in which the communication of letters is achieved by taps on the hand. Sighted people are encouraged to take a copy of the Deafblind Alphabet (shown below), to learn for possible use in the future.

www.deafblind.com

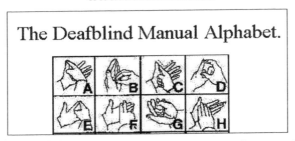

The Deafblind Web site also discusses other methods of communication, such as sign language and Braille implemented by touching on the hand.

RNID - The Royal National Institute for Deaf People

This is the largest charity representing 9 million deaf and hard of hearing people in the UK. The Web site contains news and information on topics such as hearings aids, technology, tinnitus and useful links. RNID also provides services such as **typetalk** in which a fast typist enters the text of a telephone conversation for a deaf person to read. There is an online shop and information about fundraising, campaigning issues and activities for volunteers.

www.rnid.org.uk

Getting a Hearing Aid

In the UK you can obtain a hearing aid free on the NHS or buy one from a private dispenser. The reasons for buying a hearing aid might include avoiding an NHS waiting list in a particular area. Alternatively you might want a type of hearing aid not available on the NHS. A search like the one shown below should provide all the information you need.

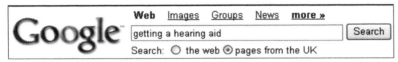

As shown in the extract below, the results include the major charities such as **RNID** and **Help the Aged**, as well as Government departments and private companies selling hearing aids.

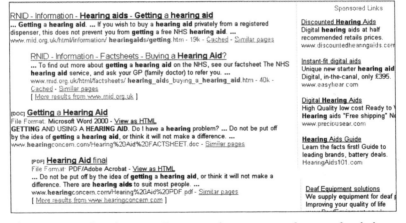

The **RNID** site has a 7-page document about obtaining hearing aids. This discusses the NHS versus private issue and also the **Hearing Aid Council Code of Practice** for hearing aid dispensers.

www.rnid.org.uk

11 Help and Support

Directgov

This is a Web site covering the whole range of Government services and information available to the public, including sections for the Over 50s and disabled people.

© Crown Copyright

There are links to articles and advice on a number of important topics such as crime prevention, independent living, caring, winter fuel payments, advice on heating your home and adaptations for special needs. There is also advice on benefits aimed at older people, motoring advice and details of the Blue Badge Scheme giving car parking help for disabled people.

Links for this section

▸ Winter Fuel Payments

▸ Sheltered housing

▸ Social services

▸ Crime prevention

▸ Improving your home

www.direct.gov.uk

disability

This is the name of a Government Web site designed to help disabled people find out about their rights and to provide helpful information about a wide range of issues affecting disabled people. Legal matters, such as the Disability Discrimination Act are discussed in detail on the **disability** Web site. There are also links to **Directgov**, as discussed earlier, which provides information on the complete range of Government services.

The **Useful Links** feature on the **disability** site gives access to many relevant Web sites such as the Disability Conciliation Services, the Disability Rights Commission, and The Mobility and Inclusion Unit. Also included is a link to Remploy which provides employment opportunities for people with a wide range of disabilities.

www.disability.gov.uk

Disabled United

This Web site describes itself as a meeting place for the disabled. There are opportunities to chat with like-minded people online and to take part in forums. The **Travel** section contains holiday accommodation for disabled people and their friends, family and carers. These include holiday cottages with good wheelchair access, for example. There is also a **Friends and Dating** service, at the time of writing containing over 4000 personal profiles. To participate, you need to become a member with your own password

The **Press Room** includes, for example, an article about a television company seeking eight disabled people for an expedition across Nicaragua.

www.disabledunited.com

Mobility

For information about the whole range of mobility aids, such as wheelchairs, stairlifts, car adaptations and orthopaedic equipment enter the keyword **mobility** into a search engine such as Google, as shown below.

The result of this search, shown below, is a list of links to companies and organizations providing mobility goods and services.

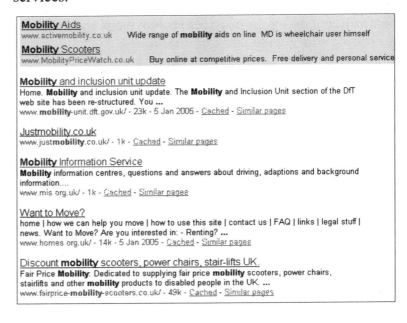

Some of the Web sites shown in the above list are described on the following pages.

RDK Mobility

This is a company supplying the complete range of mobility aids such as motorized scooters, wheelchairs, ramps, stairlifts and orthopaedic products such as neck collars and supports for knees, wrists and ankles. Car adaptations include a rotating seat as shown in the extract below. There are also hand controls for the accelerator and brakes and hoists to enable wheelchairs to be lifted into a car more easily.

www.rdkmobility.co.uk

Home | View Cart | Checkout | Search |

Bariatric

Baths & Bathlifts

Beds & Accessories

Car Adaptations

Chairs/Riser Recliners

Clothing/Footware

Computers

Continence Care

General Aids

Moving & Handling

Orthopaedic

CAR ADAPTATIONS

Save £1000's when adaptations are made by us to new vehicles prior to the vehicle being registered. Once adapted the vehicle can be purchased VAT FREE eg adapting a £15000 car would save over £2000 on VAT – you would therefore pay less than £12800 for the vehicle. This allows you £2200 to spend before being 'out of pocket'.

Rotating Car Seat

Our UK manufacturers are the worlds largest producer of rotating replacement car seats having manufactured over 3000 seats since providing the worlds 1st model over 25 years ago.

Artificial Limbs

There are several Web sites for companies manufacturing or supplying artificial limbs, including Dorset Orthopaedic shown below.

www.dorset-ortho.co.uk

Home Security

Many people these days are worried about the possibility of their home being burgled or bogus callers pretending to be from the police or one of the utility suppliers such as gas, water or electricity. To find out about help to protect your home you might enter keywords such as **home security** into a search engine such as Google.

An extract from the results of this search is shown below.

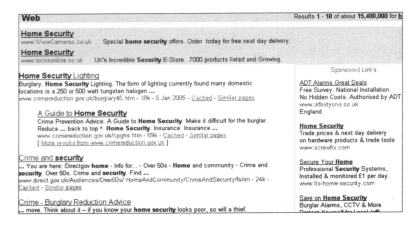

Many of the results of the search are links to commercial companies supplying home security equipment such as burglar alarms, CCTV cameras, external lighting and steel doors. However, there are also links to Government Web sites such as Directgov and the Home Office, which provide free advice on home security.

Directgov

The **Over 50s** section of the Directgov Web site gives information on crime prevention and there is advice on joining a local **Neighbourhood Watch** scheme. There is also a **Victim Support** Web site and advice for dealing with possible bogus callers and con-men, etc.

www.direct.gov.uk

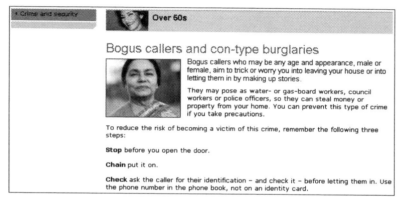

▸ Crime and security

Over 50s

Bogus callers and con-type burglaries

Bogus callers who may be any age and appearance, male or female, aim to trick or worry you into leaving your house or into letting them in by making up stories.

They may pose as water- or gas-board workers, council workers or police officers, so they can steal money or property from your home. You can prevent this type of crime if you take precautions.

To reduce the risk of becoming a victim of this crime, remember the following three steps:

Stop before you open the door.

Chain put it on.

Check ask the caller for their identification – and check it – before letting them in. Use the phone number in the phone book, not on an identity card.

© Crown Copyright

The Home Office

This Web site has a very helpful section on **Burglary Reduction Advice**. There is a comprehensive checklist of things to do to make your home more secure, such as fitting deadlocks to all outside doors and key-operated locks on all windows. The section **Extra precautions for older people** includes getting a personal alarm in case you fall. Older people are advised to use a bank account rather than keeping large amounts of cash in the home. There is also a list of steps for dealing with callers at the doorstep to ensure they are not bogus.

www.homeoffice.gov.uk

The Association of Retired and Persons Over 50

This is a not-for-profit social and campaigning organization dedicated to the older generation. The Web site covers the whole range of issues relevant to older people including **benefits, health, legal** (organizing your future), **pensions** and **links** to other not-for-profit organizations. The feature **your home** includes sections on **Home Security**, **Safety in the Home**, **Personal Security** and **Doorstep Callers**.

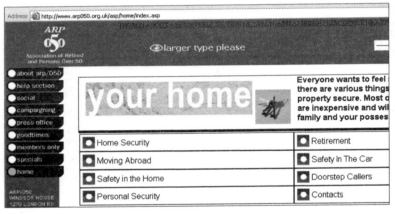

The section **Home Security** has a very comprehensive and useful list of sensible precautions which you can take, most of which are quite inexpensive. Less obvious ploys include gravel paths and prickly bushes under windows and allowing a neighbour to park their car in your drive while you're away from home. Also lopping off branches of trees which might give access to windows and applying anti-climb paint to drainpipes. The **Personal Security** section gives advice about the dangers of fire and electrical faults in the home. For anyone with difficulty reading, there is an accessibility option **larger type please**, as shown above.

www.arp050.org.uk

Appendix: List of Helpful Web Sites

It's not possible to list every single Web site which may be helpful to older people, but I hope the following will provide some useful starting points. Simply type the address into a Web browser such as Internet Explorer. There's no need to bother with the "**http://**" part which often precedes a Web address.

Welcome to MSN.co.uk - Microsoft Internet Explorer

File   Edit   View   Favorites   Tools   Help

Back   Forward   Stop   Refresh   Home

Address   www.helptheaged.org.uk

Sites Giving Wide-Ranging Support for Older People

www.helptheaged.org.uk	Campaigning charity
www.ace.org.uk	Age Concern Charity
www.adviceguide.org.uk	The Citizen's Advice Bureau
www.arp050.org.uk	Association of Retired and Persons Over 50
www.direct.gov.uk	Wide ranging Gov. Advice
www.laterlife.com	News and information
www.sixtyplusurfers.co.uk	Magazine for "seniors"
www.cennet.co.uk	Information on many topics
www.silversurfers.net	Gateway to the Internet
www.seniorsnetwork.co.uk	Over 50s info. resource
www.bbc.co.uk	Source of news and info.
www.seniority.co.uk	Over 50s online community

Pensions and Benefits

www.pensionguide.gov.uk	Gov. information
www.pensionsadvisoryservice.org.uk	
www.pensions-ombudsman.org.uk	
www.thepensionservice.gov.uk	
www.direct.gov.uk	Range of Gov. advice
www.stakeholderhelpline.org.uk	
www.fos.org.uk	Financial Ombudsman
www.dwp.gov.uk	
www.benefitsnow.co.uk	Allowances info.
www.benefitsandwork.co.uk	Free guides
www.bhas.org.uk	Benefits advice

Personal Finance

www.myfinances.co.uk	
www.thisismoney.co.uk	
www.fsa.gov.uk	Financial Services Authority
www.fool.co.uk	The Motley Fool
www.adviceonline.co.uk	
www.1stop-finance.co.uk	
www.moneyexpert.com	
www.moneyextra.com	
www.money.guardian.co.uk	

Healthy Living

www.nutrition.org.uk	British Nutrition Foundation
www.diet-i.com	Weight loss diets
www.food.gov.uk	The Food Standards Agency
www.eatwell.gov.uk	
www.wildblueberries.com	
www.dorset-blueberry.com	
www.weightwatchers.co.uk	
www.shapeup.org	Achieve a healthy weight
www.laterlifetraining.co.uk	Exercise for older people
www.bupa.co.uk	
www.netdoctor.co.uk	Online medical advice
www.patient.co.uk	Section on Seniors' Health
www.bhf.org.uk	British Heart Foundation
www.hyp.ac.uk	British Hypertension Society
www.dh.gov.uk	Department of Health
www.nhsdirect.nhs.uk	NHS Direct
www.nhs.uk	NHS Gateway
www.surgerydoor.co.uk	Online medical advice
www.ask-the-doc.com	Online medical advice
www.alcoholics-anonymous.org.uk	
www.alcoholconcern.org.uk	
www.downyourdrink.org.uk	
www.portmangroup.org.uk	Responsible drinking
www.bhf.org.uk/smoking	Giving up smoking
www.click2quit.com	

www.ageing.org	Research into Ageing
www.diabetes.org.uk	
www.parkinsons.org.uk	
www.alzheimers.co.uk	

Help for Disabled People

www.dlcc.org.uk	Try out special equipment
www.dlff.org.uk	Disabled equipment database
www.bcodp.org.uk	British Council of Disabled People
www.rnib.org.uk	Royal National Institute of the Blind
www.rnid.org.uk	Royal National Institute for Deaf People
www.deafblind.com	Deafblind Manual Alphabet
www.disability.gov.uk	Government Web site
www.disabledunited.com	Online meeting place
www.rdkmobility.co.uk	Mobility aids, wheelchairs, scooters, stairlifts, ramps, etc.
www.ddmc.org.uk	Disabled Drivers Motor Club
www.dda.org.uk	Disabled Drivers Association
www.abilitynet.org.uk	Help with computer usage

Travel Discounts

www.railcard.co.uk   Discounted train fares

www.disabledpersons-railcard.co.uk

www.senior-railcard.co.uk

www.nationalexpress.com   Discounted coach travel

Help With Housing Needs

www.energywatch.org.uk   Advice on heating

www.staywarm.co.uk   60+ Powergen scheme

www.leonard-cheshire.org   Residential homes

www.independentage.org.uk   Low-income financial help

www.cel.co.uk/foundations   Home adaptations

www.homeoffice.gov.uk   The Home Office

www.ship-ltd.org   Equity release safeguards

www.findaproperty.com   Housing options

Also consult the Web site of your local town, borough or county council on matters such as housing and social services. Enter the council name into your search engine, as shown below for Hampshire County Council.

Legal Affairs

www.lawpack.co.uk	Making a will online
www.tenminutewill.co.uk	
www.bigissuelists.co.uk	Dealing with a death
www.uk-funerals.co.uk	UK Funeral Directors
www.inlandrevenue.gov.uk	
www.taxcafe.co.uk	Inheritance tax advice
www.courtservice.gov	Probate applications

Employment and Learning

www.over50.gov.uk	New Deal 50 Plus
www.primeiniative.org.uk	Cash for 50+ entrepreneurs
www.agepositive.gov.uk	Tackling age discrimination
www.hairnet.org	Over 50s computer training
www.niace.org.uk	Older and Bolder – Learning help and links for seniors

Search Engines

www.google.co.uk	
uk.yahoo.com	
www.ask.com	Ask Jeeves
www.excite.com	
www.altavista.com	
www.lycos.com	

Adobe PDF Reader

www.adobe.co.uk	Free software for reading documents and official booklets downloaded from the Internet

Index